Making Unions Unnecessary

Charles L. Hughes

John Wiley & Sons, Inc.
New York · Chichester · Brisbane · Toronto · Singapore

This text is printed on acid-free paper.

Copyright © 1990 by John Wiley & Sons, Inc.

All rights reserved. Published simultaneously in Canada.

Reproduction or translation of any part of this work beyond that
permitted by Section 107 or 108 of the 1976 United States Copyright
Act without the permission of the copyright owner is unlawful.
Requests for permission or further information should be addressed
to the Permissions Department, John Wiley & Sons, Inc.

This publication is designed to provide accurate and authoritative
information in regard to the subject matter covered. It is said with
the understanding that the publisher is not engaged in rendering legal,
accounting, or other professional services. If legal advice or other expert
assistance is required, the services of a competent professional person
should be sought.

ISBN: 0-471-11276-3

Printed in the United States of America

10 9 8 7 6 5 4 3 2 1

FOREWORD

Once upon a time there was a King who possessed the gift of foresight. His kingdom was small but self-sufficient, and his subjects were industrious.

One night the King dreamed his kingdom was attacked by a foreign army. Because they were surprised and had little protection, the King's people were defeated and the kingdom fell quickly. The King awakened in a cold sweat and determined the kingdom must do something to protect itself.

He decided they should build a stone wall around the entire kingdom. Realizing the sacrifices his subjects would have to make to build such a wall, he knew he must convince them it was essential. Other than his older, more-experienced knights, none of his subjects had ever seen a stone fortress.

The King could not decide how to convince his people of the need for a stone wall. He rode alone into the forest to think, and after many hours of deliberation, found five possible approaches:

1. He could change the values or priorities of his individual subjects by changing the societal values of the kingdom over time. He could influence people through religious services, social rituals and kingdom schools. This would work, but it would take at least a decade and the King could not wait that long.

2. He could change the values of the young by putting them through special orientation and training classes. He could start with his army and then devise programs that all young men and women would be required to attend. Those who did not conform would be punished. This approach, too, would work, but it would take several years for any noticeable change. He didn't know how hard it would be to change strong values instituted by societal and parental conditioning, and the thought of forced learning did not appeal to him.

3. He could screen out and ostracize or exile those who would not accept the building of the wall. But he worried that if he lost key knights and artisans, the kingdom would be weakened and become easier prey. It would also reduce the

          number of people available to build the wall. Finally, he detested the thought of coercion.
4.   He could change his mind about the wall and come up with another means of self-defense. His people might find a moat or a wooden stockade more acceptable. But the King knew there was not enough water for a moat and that they'd have to chop down the entire forest for a wooden stockade (and that could be easily burned).
5.   He could explain his dream to his subjects and tell them how strongly he felt about protecting the kingdom. His knights and skilled craftsworkers were experienced enough to determine various alternatives. The King reasoned he would most likely gain greater loyalty and acceptance from his subjects if he let them decide how to protect the kingdom. The King knew this would work best with his subjects, but he was convinced the stone wall was the best means of protection.

    After much agony, the King decided to use the last approach. He rode back to his castle and asked his scribe to announce a kingdom meeting. After the people assembled, he told them of his dream and how it concerned him. He then told them he was convinced the kingdom needed to better protect itself.

    "As your King, I must guide you and protect you, but I cannot do it alone," he told them. "We must do something, but I am not certain what is best. I suggest our most experienced knights and artisans meet to determine how to best protect our kingdom. They will meet today and present a solution by sunset tomorrow."

    The King arranged for the knights and craftspeople to meet in his royal chambers and gave them whatever they needed to be comfortable. He was tempted to tell them he was convinced they should build a stone wall, but he remained silent and paced the royal garden while waiting for their call.

    The next day a trusted knight stepped forth from the chambers and asked for the King. When the King entered the chambers, the knight announced, "Great King, we have decided something must be done to protect ourselves and our future generations. We have decided we need to build a stone wall around the kingdom."

    The King joined his people at the chamber table. "Tell me why you decided on a stone wall," he said, and they began convincing the King of the merit of their decision.

    And the King smiled. . . .

ACKNOWLEDGMENTS

Thanks to Lew Abrams for his continued support, and to Wayne Wright of CVR for his significant contributions to the industry and this book.

PREFACE

Eliminating the Negatives

No organization is completely free of problems. To be so may be an admirable goal, but it is not a particularly realistic one. It is not the absence of problems, but the absence of unidentified and unresolved problems that sets superior organizations apart from the rest. An environment where everyone works in concert to reinforce and eliminate the negatives that are certain to appear from time to time is the only environment that has any hope of achieving excellence. Minor irritants become major, and numerous irritants of any size that affect large numbers of employees become more of a concern than the achievement of organizational goals. Attempts to revitalize the organization or its individual workgroups will fail without first eliminating the negatives.

Over and over, we see the manifestation of this phenomenon without clearly understanding the causes. How many times have management groups tried to borrow very successful processes, like quality circles, only to have them fall flat in the new environment? The result should have been predictable. The management response is also too often predictable: "Quality circles are a farce—they caused more harm than good before we dropped them." Recent studies have estimated that as many as 60 percent of the companies that attempt to implement a quality circles program fail. Others, using the exact same approach, report real, measurable successes in productivity, quality and cost reductions. The losers do not understand that the fault is not in the instrument but in the environment, and they continue the search for some other quick fix or gimmick to leapfrog them ahead of the pack. First, we must analyze and understand the major causes of high levels of employee dissatisfaction. Only then can we identify corrective actions to eliminate these barriers and begin the process of building the kinds of organizations that our employees, customers and stockholders deserve.

Studies over the past twenty years involving thousands of employees in hundreds of organizations have been conducted by the Center for Values Research (CVR), and the underlying issues responsible for both favorable and unfavorable attitudes toward the work environment have been identified. By this process, eight initial areas have been identified by employees as having major impact on their day-to-day existence. (These are by no means all of the factors, but do represent the primary problem areas because they address a critical issue and/or because they represent areas of significant unfavorable response in organizations throughout the U.S. and Canada.) The negatives, in no particular order, are:

- Lack of pride in the organization
- Concern over job security
- No trust in supervisors
- Feeling of favoritism
- Little cooperation between groups
- Insufficient communication/information
- Low perceptions about equity in pay
- Lack of confidence in management.

The concepts and systems of management by objectives have a role in the maintenance of unionfree status. Management by objectives theory prescribes that the key elements of the organization be identified as specific goals to be achieved or maintained. If it is important to the organization to operate without unions, then this objective deserves the same consideration, planning, and commitment as objectives relating to sales, profits, and return on assets. The financial aspects of the corporation are documented, and resources are committed to the attainment of those goals. Organizations make no secret of their intent in the economic arena. A study of organizations that have remained unionfree shows that they have applied management by objectives to the concept of unions and human resources practices with the same vigor that is typically afforded to other aspects of the business. The concepts and strategic approaches leading to the attainment of the "goal: no unions" is the topic of this book.

Based on material from *East Meets West* by Wayne L. Wright, CVR Dallas, Texas, 1987.

ABOUT THE AUTHOR

Charles L. Hughes, Ph.D.

Dr. Hughes is best known for his leadership in the unionfree movement in America. His book, *Goal Setting: Key to Individual and Organizational Effectiveness*, won the McKinsey Award for Excellence and was the first existential concept of management published. *Making Unions Unnecessary* set forth the original philosophy that "any management that gets a union deserves it." His latest books are *Union free: A Systematic Approach* and *The Generic Handbook*. His long-running seminar, "How to Be Unionfree," continues as the foundation for positive employee relations. He also pioneered the use of attitude surveys with the emphasis on employee involvement in making positive changes.

Dr. Hughes is president of the Center for Values Research (CVR), which he cofounded with Vincent Flowers in Dallas in 1974. Dr. Hughes served as Corporate Consultant on organizational development for IBM for five years and worked ten years with Texas Instruments in several roles, including Corporate Director of Personnel. He holds a Ph.D. from the University of Houston and M.S. and B.A. degrees from Southern Methodist University.

CVR

The Center for Values Research (CVR) is an employee relations consulting group located in Dallas, Texas. Its staff conducts workshops on remaining unionfree and other issues, consults on employee relations practices and helps companies to improve productivity, surveys employee attitudes, conducts research on human value systems, and publishes materials to help companies in all these areas.

CVR believes in balancing the goals of the organization and the needs of the employees, and that the materialistic goal of increasing productivity and the humanistic goals of meeting people's needs are not incongruent or mutually exclusive. Rather, these goals are synergistic. Third-party intervention is unnecessary when management understands and responds positively to the different value systems and needs of employees, and when communications are direct, open, and honest.

CONTENTS

I. **The Positive Approach**
  1. The Positive Approach 3
  2. Teaching People to Join Unions 5
  3. Goal: No Unions 7
  4. Overcoming Barriers to Productivity 13

II. **Strategic Approaches to Making Unions Unnecessary**
  5. Strategic Approaches to Making Unions Unnecessary 23
  6. Employee Attitudes 35
  7. Employee Value Systems 53
  8. Job Design 71
  9. Management Systems and Procedures 81
  10. Growth Opportunity and Advancement 87
  11. Pay and Benefits 101
  12. Equal Employment Opportunity 121
  13. Facilities and Job Security 123
  14. Making Unions Unnecessary 127

III. **Appendixes**
  A. Self-Audits 131
  B. A Comparison of Responses to Employee Attitudes Survey 145
  C. What Causes Poor Attitudes—A Checklist of Typical Employee Complaints 147
  D. A Checklist of Ownership Process Ideas 151
  E. A Checklist for Your Pay System 155
  F. The Ingredients of a Pay System 157

IV. **References**

I

THE POSITIVE APPROACH

CHAPTER 1

THE POSITIVE APPROACH

After three decades of declining membership, unions have begun to look at themselves and their relationship with their potential members. For example, while manufacturing union membership slides down, the white collar membership as a percentage of the workforce is accelerating. This follows the shift from manufacturing to service employment.

In times past a person or an institution could hold the same beliefs, pursue the same objectives, work the same strategies and follow the same tactics for a lifetime. With the rise of the unionfree movement during the past fifteen years, many organizations have truly made unions unnecessary by making them obsolete. Over 80 percent of the workforce is working unionfree.

Some unions, as with some businesses, will cease to exist because they could not respond appropriately. However, many will survive, and other unions, new, better-managed and -led ones, will be created to take the place of the deceased. Except, that is, where better-managed and -led businesses do all of the things unions are purported to do for employees, and remove the need for third-party representation. Many have accomplished this task; others are trying.

Unfortunately, many managers think unions are no longer a force in America, so they need to do little to become world-class employers. This is where revitalized unions will make their move. So the first question management might ask is this: Do we really want to be unionfree, and why? (See Appendix A, Self-Audit 1.)

Any management that gets a union deserves it—and they get the kind they deserve. No labor union has ever captured a group of employees without the full cooperation and encouragement of managers who create the need for unionization. Management language does not even have a positive word for operating unionfree.

A great deal has been written about the evils of unions; as much has been written about the decadence of management. It is futile to try to assign guilt to either party. This is a negative approach, and today positive approaches are required. Prolabor or promanagement arguments only serve to continue an adversary process in which evidence and rhetoric can be mustered on either side and only emotional satisfaction is accomplished. We no longer need the antiunion, procompany dichotomy that has persisted; business, industry, and society today need positive responses to pressing needs.

Union leaders have always claimed that joining a union will make employees happier because it will provide them with better pay and benefits, more job security, less favoritism, and more consistency. Study data clearly shows that union employees are *not* more satisfied than unionfree employees; they are *less* satisfied. This holds true regardless of age, sex, race, length of service or education (See Appendix B for study results).

The positive approach is this: *Make unions unnecessary.* The need for unions has its origin in people's concern for job security and their rights, both as human beings and as members of an organization who are paid to perform tasks. When management begins with the traditional assumption that there is a gap between "management" and "labor," that gap will surely appear. It begins in the minds of managers and eventually permeates the thinking of everyone, as well as the policies and procedures by which the institution is operated. The split created in concept becomes reality.

The positive approach contends that unionization is not inevitable if management conducts the business in a way that makes labor unions unnecessary in the first place. There is no compulsion in human behavior requiring people to join unions. The vast majority of employees in the United States are not members of unions. But the less than 20 percent minority who do carry union cards influence industries critical to the economic system.

Unions are expensive. In several comparisons of union and unionfree facilities, the payroll and benefits costs of unionized companies average 20 percent more than those of unionfree companies or the unionfree facilities of companies that have both labor organizations and unionfree operations. This cost is not primarily in individual wages and benefits, but results from redundant employees, narrowly defined jobs, restrictive production, strikes, and slowdowns. What is more, some studies indicate that product quality and customer satisfaction is significantly better in unionfree operations. The costs are the price of inefficiency and ineffectiveness. The tragedy is that the money does not go to workers. With a few exceptions, employees within a given industry earn about the same rates of pay whether they are union members or not. Many unionfree companies keep their wages in line with unionized companies, and most partially unionized corporations match unionfree wages to their labor contracts. The money involved in the additional costs that result from the presence of labor unions is mostly lost in lower productivity: Union members lose, company management loses, and the consumer loses.

CHAPTER 2

TEACHING PEOPLE TO JOIN UNIONS

The management of many organizations can legitimately be said to have trained their employees to form unions and engage in collective activity. Perhaps an analogy will illustrate the point. This analogy can be called the "jelly bean theory." If we were to go to Yellowstone National Park and stop our automobile, one of the natural consequences would be for a bear to approach the car. If the driver rolls down the window, the bear will look inward expectantly. If we give the bear a jelly bean, it is natural for her to expect a second jelly bean, because she has just been rewarded for approaching the car. If we give the bear another jelly bean, she has learned that as long as she glares at us she is reinforced for her behavior. If we continue this process long enough, we will run out of jelly beans, at which time the bear will take not only the empty sack but an arm and other parts of our anatomy as well.

We are likely to wonder why that lovable bear has suddenly turned into a hostile animal. The answer is simple: The bear has been rewarded and reinforced for her aggressive activities, in much the same manner that employees of some organizations have been rewarded for collective activity. How many times have corporations failed to pay the standard rate for a job in a community until the employees banded together and raised a hue and cry that resulted in management's giving the needed increase? How many times have employees asked for job security and fair treatment, only to be ignored until they engaged in concerted collective activity? Surely, many employees have been trained to engage in aggressive behavior toward the management of a corporation because this is the only way in which they got a response.

It is not simply because of neglect and poor management that employees of corporations feel the need to form and join unions; it goes even further, to the point where some employees have found that the only way they receive proper treatment is collective activity, for which they are rewarded and reinforced.

Summary and Key Points

In contrast to the "win-lose" approach often taken in management-labor relations, a "win-win" system can make unions unnecessary. It is of no avail to debate the pros and cons of unions or unionism, any more than it is to attempt to identify who is at fault and who is most heroic—corporations or unions. Our approach is neither procompany nor antiunion, but rather propeople.

We further believe that the majority of corporations have, in fact, taught their people to join and form unions—because that is the only way they get a response—instead of committing themselves to dealing with people as effectively as possible so that the dichotomy between management and labor does not arise in the first place. The basic concept, therefore, is "make unions unnecessary"—that is, use preventive maintenance rather than after-the-fact firefighting.

CHAPTER 3

GOAL: NO UNIONS

Sitting on a one-legged stool is possible, but tricky. Superior balance is required, and the slightest tilt yields a crash. Sitting on a two-legged stool is possible and not quite as tricky, but still difficult. A move in the wrong direction results in a frantic rebalancing act or another crash. That is why stools are built three-legged. (Everyone knows the tripod is a very stable design.) So it is with the management of an organization—or needs to be.

Unfortunately, most managers today are expected to balance on one-legged or two-legged stools. The first leg is invariably financial performance. Managers must depend only on "bottom line" assessment of their performance. To attain the rewards contingent on the satisfaction of financial goals, their roles become exclusively one-legged. Those are the rules. In some organizations, managers' goals, roles, rules and rewards have a second leg to contend with—customer satisfaction. They must balance both financial satisfaction and customer satisfaction to receive an acceptable assessment of their performance. But what about the third leg—employee satisfaction, which is vital to the maintenance of unionfree status? If managers were required to achieve positive employee relations as well as positive financial and customer results, would it not change their behavior? Would it not yield a more balanced organization? Would they not manage to pursue all three goals, fulfill all three roles, live within all three sets of rules, and gain personal rewards as a result?

Balancing Our Concerns

The Center for Values Research (CVR) proposes, therefore, that your organization adopt the three-legged stool model of an organization and hold managers accountable for employee satisfaction along with financial performance and customer satisfaction.

How might this be accomplished? You already have the first leg, financial satisfaction. You may even have the second leg, customer satisfaction. If not, better start thinking about it. Customer satisfaction could take the shape of quality of product or service as measured by a survey of customers. Go ask the customers what they think about the managers' performance in a way that can be quantified, just as we quantify financial matters.

To measure employee satisfaction, go ask the employees how well managers are performing in a way that can be quantified. This leg easily takes the shape of an attitude survey. Then we can measure all three legs of the stool and expect balanced performance. If one of the legs is too short or too long, the organization will be out of balance and so will management behavior.

The system for assessment of managerial performance should be tied to performance appraisal and subsequent rewards. Conversely, failure to perform in a balanced way must result in reduced rewards. Continued unbalanced performance will result in "career rearrangement" or out-placement to a competitor.

Surely some managers already take the three-legged stool approach, either because they are intuitively balanced in an existential way, or because the reward system clearly indicates such behavior is desirable. Even if the intuitive comprehension is not there, continued reinforcement of the appropriate behavior will ultimately result in deeper understanding. For those managers who do not behave in an appropriately balanced manner, a clear system of goals, roles, rules and rewards will elicit positive responses. This permits us to sort out those who "can and will" from those who "can but will not" and those who simply "cannot."

Objectives, Strategies and Tactics:
A Generic Planning Model

If you do not care where you are going, any path will get you there. To take steps along a path is progress only if we are going in a desired direction. That is simple enough a concept to understand when we are walking. It seems to be absent when we are designing human resource policies and practices. All too often we get confused in selecting among various approaches to designing a system for pay, benefits, hiring, promotion, training, structure and all the rest. The reason for the muddle is obvious. If we do not care about or do not know our ultimate objective, then there is no basis for choosing among alternatives. The question is, what are we trying to accomplish? (Also obvious, but often ignored.) So, here is a Generic Planning Model we call Objectives, Strategies and Tactics, or OST.

Tactical matters come last, strategies in the middle, and objectives first. The confusion is that typically the tactical planning comes first, then we create a strategy and hope it fits with some unspecified objective. An objective is the overall direction we want to go in employee relations. It is the human resource philosophy for the entire organization. Until managers have specified the guiding principles for the overall mission of the human resources aspects of the business, we should not make any attempts or spend any energy trying to figure out what to do strategically or tactically. The objectives, therefore, are the general direction we wish to go. They state the "Whats?"

Objectives are the responsibility of the "higher levels" of the organization, usually referred to as management. Strategies are the responsibility of the mid-level managers and supervisors. Tactics permit and encourage the participation of other employees in the selection among alternative, more specific, and detailed steps along the strategic path toward the objective.

- An objective could be "manage people in a way that permits and encourages learning to do more, and thus to contribute more."
- The strategy, then, might be "design a pay system that rewards versatility, adaptability and broad-based skills."
- One tactic possible is "increase pay proportionate with acquiring multiple skills, willingly applying them in a variety of tasks."

The Need for Commitment

The objective we address here, then, is the maintenance of a unionfree organization. Obviously, most companies would prefer to operate without a union. However, many of them fail to document their objective as a policy statement written and signed by the chief executive officer. One might ask why, if the organization is truly committed to operating without a union, it is necessary to have a written document stating that intent. The reasons that a clear, concise statement of the position regarding unions is necessary are the same reasons that other management objectives are stated: commitment and communication. To maintain unionfree status, it may be necessary to reorganize major portions of the organization and its human resources policies and practices. A statement of the guiding principle and objective is necessary to give clarity to the direction and unanimity to the company's efforts and allocation of resources. This is particularly true with regard to organizations that are decentralized and have branch plants and offices located in remote regions of the United States. This management document is much too important simply to be kept in a file or in a corporate organization manual. It should be disseminated throughout the entire workforce, from top management to supervision to rank-and-file employees.

The place for stating the position on unions is in the employee handbook, an important publication that serves many purposes. If an organization is willing to commit itself to the public and to its employees in writing, there will be no question in anyone's mind about where the organization stands and why certain actions are being taken. This also gives the organization the opportunity to explain many policies and practices in advance of union organizing activity, so that there is no question later that management is devising new strategies and tactics simply for the purpose of blocking a union organizing drive. Therefore, a basic question that management must ask itself is, "Do all our employees, from the top to the bottom of the organizational hierarchy, understand our policy as regards unions, and have we communicated it to them by both written and oral means?"

Some managements are reluctant to communicate their position on unions in the belief that mentioning unions may give rise to union activity. They feel that some things are best left unsaid, because people may begin to wonder why the organization is so concerned with unions and whether employees may have something to fear from the corporation. If management is willing to assume that everything is completely in order throughout the organization so that there is no possibility of union activity, then it is conceivable that the company position on unions need not be stated for the employees to read or hear. However, few managements can make such a sweeping assumption. Further, in the best of organizations, there are problems from time to time. Management may not abuse all of the people all of the time but certainly will abuse some of them some of the time and, in too many instances, all of the people some of the time. There is far more to be gained by going on public record with the company's philosophy and policy regarding unions well in advance of an organizing drive than there is to be feared from causing commotion and concern by statements that are communicated.

The following episode has been repeated in a number of organizations. During an organizing drive, management felt that it was necessary to communicate, for the first time, its position on unions. This was done in a group meeting in which the top manager called the employees together to discuss the company's philosophy and policy about unions. In each of these cases, the same scenario was played: At the conclusion of the talk about why the company felt that unions were not necessary in order for everyone to get fair treatment and due process, the inside employee-organizer was accused by other employees of having perpetrated a hoax. For the first time, employees realized that management did not want a union. The message being disseminated by the inside organizer was that management did not care and possibly even favored unionization. In each of these instances, the inside organizer terminated his activities voluntarily.

Some managements have been reluctant to take a public position for fear that somehow an unfair labor practice may be involved. As long as it is simply a statement of the company's position that unions are unnecessary, no coercion or threat is involved, and no action is taken against any individual or group of employees for acting in behalf of the union, there are no legal restrictions on the organization. (Of course, a union may allege that an unfair labor practice has been committed, but there is a big difference between allegation and fact.)

There are, however, matters of timing and phrasing. It has generally been found to be more effective to make the unionfree policy statement well in advance of any organizing activity, because to issue such a position paper or speech after an organizing drive has commenced lends credence to the union's position that the company employees are being intimidated. As for phrasing, credibility is the key word. The statement should acknowledge that the company, like any human organization, is not perfect, and that problems exist. But it should also state the company's belief that outside intervention, in the form of unionization, will not help to resolve those problems and may make it more difficult for management to deal equitably with the employees.

Here is an example of such a statement of policy that is both given orally and printed in employee handbooks in one of the largest unionfree corporations in the United States: "We prefer to deal with people directly rather than through a third party. This is a nonunion organization. It always has been, and it is certainly our desire that it always be that way. This does not mean that from time to time we do not have problems. However, we have always been able to work these out among ourselves without the intervention of outsiders. No organization is free from day-to-day problems, but we believe that we have policies and practices to help resolve problems rather than fight with each other. Unions have never gotten anyone a job; neither have they caused anybody to keep a job. Only all of us working together to make this a viable, healthy organization are able to do that. We encourage you to bring your problems to your supervisor or anyone else you feel can help you, and we, in turn, promise to listen and give the best possible response that we can. In today's world there are many pressures. We want to keep our organization free from artificially created tensions that can be brought on by the intervention of outsiders, such as a union. We feel that a union would be of no advantage to any of us. It would hurt the business on which we all depend for our livelihood. We accept our responsibility to provide the best working conditions, pay, and benefits that we can afford. It is not necessary for you to pay union dues to receive fair treatment in this company. Each of you is an individual, and you have the right to speak for yourself."

Some organizations go further in their statement on unions, adding a paragraph about union authorization cards. Some unionfree organizations phrase it this way: "If anyone should come to you and ask you to sign a union authorization card, we are asking you now to refuse to sign it. You have a right to join and belong to a union, and you have an equal right *not* to join and belong to a union. If any other employee should interfere or try to coerce you into signing a union authorization card, please report it to your supervisor and we will see that the harassment is stopped immediately."

Another major opportunity to communicate the company's position on unions occurs during the employment interview. Although it is considered an unfair labor practice to refuse to hire an applicant because of prior union activity, it is within the organization's rights to state its position regarding operating without a union so that individual applicants will clearly understand the nature of the organization they are likely to join. It is advisable to have this statement in writing so that applicants may read it rather than have the employment interviewer engage in dialogue with them. This minimizes the chances of an unfair labor practice charge that anyone was refused employment simply on the basis of union beliefs and prior practices. Research in the area of communication and persuasion has also shown that new employees during their orientation program, particularly in the first few hours, form lasting impressions. When an individual understands that it is a unionfree company and that the majority of the employees want it to stay that way, we have eliminated the possibility of misunderstanding and have established a concept in that individual's mind that will generally be lasting.

For a self-audit on your company's commitment to unionfree status, see Appendix A, Self-Audit 2.

Summary and Key Points

Credibility is essential; clarity is necessary. Management's candor in communicating its position on unions will generally be met with appreciation by the majority of the employees. Establishing the pattern today rather than after an organizing drive has commenced will go a long way toward shaping the attitudes and thinking of employees so that later, should an organizing drive occur, the company has established a basic theme upon which to build: Unions are not necessary in this company.

CHAPTER 4

OVERCOMING BARRIERS TO PRODUCTIVITY

Few managerial topics have generated more analysis, debate or mistakes in recent years than the so-called Japanese style of management. "So-called," because there is a strong body of evidence indicating much of what falls under this heading was adapted from Western culture.

The Japanese studied and analyzed different philosophies and techniques, sorted out what made sense in terms of their culture, and then adapted these to fit their needs. Several of the better, more successful companies in the United States have embraced these concepts for years; the primary difference is that the Japanese practice what they preach more often and with more consistency than do Americans.

Almost all of the "Japanese" practices work well in the United States, but not by using little bits here and there. A holistic approach tailored to each individual organization is necessary. For example, attempts to incorporate quality circles onto an organization burdened with negative employee attitudes and severe distrust of management consistently fail.

The Japanese characteristics of interdependence, strong familial feelings, respect for the "face" (and space) of others, and maintenance of harmony are natural results of millions of people learning to survive together on a small island with few natural resources. These traits, plus an ethnically homogeneous population with enormous behavioral sameness, characterize Japanese lives.

Conversely, Americans come from diverse ethnic backgrounds; tolerate behavioral differences; and worship freedom, individuality and the entrepreneurial spirit in a vast young country rich in natural resources. The subsequent values and behavioral differences are inevitable.

The Japanese strength comes primarily from their homogeneity and willingness to subjugate individuality to the team process. They readily identify themselves as part of a team (family, company) rather than as individuals; Japanese workers do what's good for the company even though they might be unhappy in their jobs. Behavioral controls originate not only within the individual but from peer pressure as well. Japanese management has simply *designed systems around* these predominate employee values.

American strength comes from diversity and enlightened self-interest. A willingness to be open, candid, honest and even different is a powerful force if properly channeled toward common goals. This does not mean Americans are averse to teamwork—most are not, but to put forth maximum effort, Americans must first be convinced that what's best for the team is also best for themselves.

When enlightened managers provide a positive environment in which the organization's productivity needs and the individual's personal needs are both being met, Americans actively participate in creative teamwork that surpasses the best efforts of the conformist Japanese.

American workers cannot and will not strive toward organizational excellence however until managers eliminate the barriers that frustrate their efforts.

Barriers to Productivity Take Many Shapes

Barriers are conspicuously evident in poor and mediocre organizations and noticeably absent in many of the more successful groups. Specifically, they focus on several key aspects of the organization.

• *Lack of direction.* Failure to use a systematic, strategic approach to managing human resources can create a personnel nightmare. If management wants everyone pulling in the same direction, that direction must be identified with as much detail as possible. This requires carefully designed and fully comprehended objectives and strategies—what we are trying to do, how we are going to do it, and how we know when we are succeeding.

Lacking that, there can be no clear understanding of, or commitment to, the company's objectives. The result will be much like alternate wheels in a gear box, with about half the people heading in the wrong direction—a surefire recipe for chaos.

Every organization has a psychological environment. Most, unfortunately, have evolved haphazardly, but the most effective American organizations designed their cultures ahead of time and work to that plan.

If you want excellence, you first design it, and then build it in; that is what the Japanese do so well.

Most Japanese and many successful American organizations spend most of their time analyzing *what* they are trying to accomplish rather than making quick decisions on *how* to accomplish specifics when the overall direction is unclear. (If the American railroads had understood sooner that they were not in the railroad business but the transportation industry, they would probably still be with us in strength.) Monthly, quarterly and yearly decision-making mentality and repeated changes in direction are the results of such management failure.

Managers in successful organizations set the course, analyze and approve supporting strategies, and then stay out of the detailed "how to" decisions. Top management in Japan *leads;* Americans tend to push employees.

• *Poor organizational structure.* Poor organization is a major barrier that creates negativism and divisiveness and that blocks positive communication, involvement and teamwork.

Vertically, most structures have too many levels, including management. Coupled with a mentality that requires rigid adherence to a fixed organizational structure, the result is an organization that's top heavy, inflexible, costly, and inefficient.

Based on the belief that breadth of knowledge is at least as important as depth, and maybe more so, Japanese organizations and the resultant hiring, training, and assignments are structured for maximum flexibility and versatility:

(1)   Individual jobs, including management jobs, are broadly defined.
(2)   Specialists are few and far between, and employees think of themselves as part of a company rather than part of a profession.
(3)   Trust in the individual leads to individual accountability, instead of unnecessary staff watchdogs.

Horizontally, most American organizations suffer from too many inflexible, specific job descriptions and job classifications. These contribute to inefficiency as well as to employee dissatisfaction. This is but one of the undesirable by-products of logical, digital, inflexible job evaluation systems. Detailed written job descriptions and narrowly defined job classifications ultimately serve only one purpose—to tell people what they *cannot* do. Some of the most distressing words management can ever hear are, "But, it's not my job."

Broad-based descriptions and classifications not only allow for greater efficiency and cost savings to the company, but also encourage versatility and job satisfaction for employees—a real win/win environment the Japanese know how to achieve.

Pay Systems Are Misunderstood and Perceived to be Inequitable

• *Pay and pay systems*. Far too many organizations continue to cling to systems and levels of pay that are not understood by employees, or that are understood and perceived to be unfair.

External equity is rarely a problem insofar as fairness is perceived. Internal equity more often than not, however, is a problem, and one that is completely controllable by management. Problem systems are characterized by multiplicity of pay levels or job classification structures or both and attempt to use complicated merit pay concepts. In addition, these problem systems are frequently accompanied by complex, subjective job evaluation systems (alleged to be simple and objective) that elicit zero credibility.

To almost any American observation, Japanese pay systems would be considered totally unworkable. The equal pay for equal work concept is nonexistent, having been replaced with a pay based on need.

Two individuals working side by side may be paid rates that vary 50 percent or more if one is older, has more company service, and has a large family. This system works because both individuals in this example agree that the difference is appropriate.

Any system supported by employees will work, which is what American management needs to learn.

Pay policies represent extreme examples of values bias. Compensation "experts" design systems that feel good to them, and therefore, by definition, are not understood or accepted by most others.

There seems to be an unwritten rule that says we cannot have pay systems that are simple, easy to understand and easy to administer. Instead, we have bell-shaped curves, forced distributions, matrices, and maximums, mid points, and incentives that don't exist. These barriers persist through failure to follow three simple steps. First, analyze what is to be accomplished by the pay system. Next, honestly evaluate whether these goals are appropriate and acceptable and, finally, design a simple system to attain these goals.

• *Managerial selection and training.* The most significant differences between typical American and Japanese managers are manifest in their at-work behavioral expectations.

Americans are trained that success in climbing the corporate ladder goes to those who are the most competitive, aggressive, and rational (two and two *always* equals four). Those individuals who have the right combination of these characteristics hit the "fast track" and attain increasing authority, power, and status.

The Japanese, including Japanese operations in the United States, don't even consider hiring or promoting individual superstars. They opt for those capable of being helpful, supportive and emotional leaders in a team environment (two and two equals five is OK if it works).

New graduates hired into most Japanese organizations can expect to be observed for as many as ten years before any attempt is made to designate those with managerial abilities. During that time, they are judged on their ability to cooperate—not on how competitive they can be.

Most approaches to selection, training, and promotion of managers in the U.S. are woefully lacking in the analysis of people skills. Would you hire or tolerate a secretary who could not type, or a truck driver who could not drive? Of course not. Then why do so many American managers continue to survive, receive big bonus increases, and even get promoted when they cannot effectively deal with people?

In general, performance review systems judge managerial people skills negligibly, if at all. This does not go unnoticed by the manager—you get what you pay for.

Organizations spend millions of dollars each year on training programs to teach managers how to deal effectively with people. Then they are placed in situations in which their role models in upper management contradict many of their newly learned skills. Which has more impact on their behavior in interacting effectively with those they manage? Will they believe what they see or what they hear? If *all* training programs reinforce what they teach, then managers will be appropriately trained and more sensitive to the needs of their people.

• *We/they symbols*. Glaring status symbols always have a negative effect on the workforce. The "haves" love them, but attainment of status often becomes more important than effectively pursuing the goals of the organization. The "have-nots" hate status symbols because they feel less important.

Being singled out as different, better, or special is not only not expected in the Japanese culture, it is unwanted. To be treated differently is an embarrassment and causes the recipient to "lose face." Recognition and rewards are oriented to the team, not to the individual.

In situations in which there are differences, they are typically subtle. For example, the manager of a large department would not have an ornate, separate office, but his desk may be facing a different direction.

Everyone recognizes that rank has its privileges, and that's okay. The further one advances in an organization, the more individual freedom, the more pay, the more responsibility one receives.

Unnecessary we/they divisions, however, serve no purpose except to physically or psychologically separate one group of employees from another. This occurs because outmoded assumptions imply that people cannot be important unless they look important and are treated differently and better than others. In simplest terms, we/they symbols are designed merely to feed the egos and self-importance of certain members of the organization. The assumption is that they would be less effective, particularly in management positions, without these status symbols. The truth is, they are often less effective *because* of them.

For Many Employees, Job Security Is a Tacit Concern

• *No job security*. Although not as prevalent as Americans sometimes assume, lifetime employment is a key factor in many Japanese organizations. Everyone assumes employment for the long haul and acts accordingly. Voluntary resignations are rare; involuntary terminations and layoffs are virtually unknown. With this commitment, and knowing that business cycles also exist in Japan, management uses many contract and temporary employees to absorb unpredictable swings in workforce needs to protect the permanent positions.

Lifetime employment or absolute job security for all employees in most American organizations is not realistic and isn't even desirable. For qualified employees, however, organizations need to manage their affairs to maximize long-term employment.

Job security is a key issue for many employees and although this concern is mostly unspoken, it exists and should be a primary concern of management. Unions and government agencies often assume management has no concern, and consequently external protection and limitations evolve.

Turnover is expensive and its short-term costs are obvious. Longer-term costs with regard to loss of continuity are real but less measurable. In addition, turnover not only includes indiscriminate terminations (a primary cause of employee dissatisfaction), but also includes continuous cycles of layoff, recall, layoff, ad infinitum. When employees feel, even with good performance and commitment on their part, management is not trying to avoid layoffs, significant barriers are created that keep employees from really turning on and giving total commitment.

Management commitment, manifested in long-term planning and program design, can eliminate much of this instability, even in a fluctuating market. The Japanese understand this.

• *Lack of systematic employee involvement.* Employee involvement—participative management—is probably the most important opportunity for management today. Employee involvement does not mean soft or permissive management nor does it mean decision making by popular vote. It simply means using the knowledge and experience of *all* employees when there is a reasonable expectation that those involved have the ability and desire for positive contribution. "Japanese-style management" is based on the premise that the total exceeds the sum of the individual parts.

Intelligently handled, a regular system of employee involvement can reap huge rewards for an organization. This is one of the areas where the Japanese outdo most Western organizations. A system of participative management cannot only enhance a positive employee relations environment, but also can significantly effect productivity, quality, and profitability.

Most Japanese managers have an amazing amount of patience when faced with decisions that have broad-based impact within their organizations. They continue discussion and analysis, seemingly forever, if there is significant, though minority, opposition to a plan. Most Americans find this disconcerting, preferring to get several opinions and then quickly fashion and issue a decision.

Under any system, implementers undermine decision makers when they disagree with or don't understand a decision. The Japanese eliminate this possibility by getting support and understanding before the decision is made. Ensuring that all levels of the workforce are appropriately involved in the decision-making process yields positive results in many areas. It stimulates cooperation and understanding between work groups; improves communications; and allows a systematic, broad-based analysis of what is working well and not so well, and why. The ability to achieve understanding and support of management decisions before the fact reduces time spent in retracing steps and revising decisions.

Possibly the greatest attribute of the Japanese style of management is that it develops genuine leaders rather than insensitive dictators.

• *Ill-conceived hiring/training.* Selection, hiring, and training practices based on incorrect assumptions lead to misfits, mismatches, turnover, and dissatisfaction. Too often, organizations hire employees who are incompatible with corporate culture or the work group to which they are assigned.

Typically, the amount of time, money, and effort invested in the selection process varies directly with the level of the position to be filled. For example, entry level people are often hired by the human resource department.

The immediate supervisor may meet the new employee for the first time when he or she reports for work.

Following a new-employee orientation, the employee is placed in a training program (usually on the job) and told a probationary period must be served. This probationary period theoretically serves to determine if the employee can do the job, wants to do the job, will come to work regularly and on time, has the proper attitude toward work, and is compatible with the corporate culture. If an employee fails on any of these criteria, we terminate the employee, write off the expense, trot in a new group, repeat the process, and hope for the best.

Because of the permanence of employment, the necessity for teamwork, and the unyielding dedication to quality, the Japanese are meticulous in hiring decisions and training programs. To ensure compatibility, the selection process often includes interviews with the applicant's family.

To establish quality in the workforce and overcome hiring barriers, companies must carefully detail the organization and positions, take the time necessary for thorough interviewing, and offer employment only to those who are compatible with the organization and with the work group to which they will be assigned.

Managers and supervisors must be actively involved in screening and hiring decisions. It may also be necessary to implement a preemployment training program to assess employee ability *before* the hiring decision.

Summary and Key Points

Search out all of these primary barriers to organizational effectiveness and whittle them down to size.

Get rid of out-of-date, irrelevant assumptions and design an environment that enhances and encourages excellence for the organization.

It may not be "Japanese," it may not be "textbook," it may not have ever been done before—but it *will* be an effective and rewarding undertaking.

This chapter, by Wayne L. Wright, Senior Employee Relations Consultant, CVR (1987), is reprinted with the permission of *Personnel Journal*, Costa Mesa. CA; all rights reserved.

II

STRATEGIC APPROACHES TO MAKING UNIONS UNNECESSARY

CHAPTER 5

STRATEGIC APPROACHES TO MAKING UNIONS UNNECESSARY

It is necessary but not sufficient to have an objective of maintaining unionfree status. For any goal to be reached, regardless of how committed and motivated one may be to attain it, it is necessary to have a plan of action. There must be a strategic plan for accomplishing the objective of maintaining unionfree status.

Strategies are the paths that we will take in various aspects of human resource management to move us in the direction already determined by the objectives. They address the question of "How?" Strategies define the most effective and efficient means to achieving the ultimate objectives, or at least pursuing them. They are the most creative aspect of planning, or need to be, and should be repeated, restated and repeated again, until everyone involved has psychological ownership. They are what make the organization unique, because the value systems of all members of the organization must be addressed as well as the products/services to be provided to customers and the financial objectives of the business. Strategic planning is the opportunity to balance the three-legged stool.

Tactics are the three W's: Who is going to do What, When? Tactical planning is, therefore, a significant opportunity for "appropriate" employee involvement/participation. It defines the steps along the strategic path already selected. The strategy is the basis for selecting from among the various alternatives of who, what and when. The strategies for opposing unionization may take either a negative, fire-fighting approach or a positive, preventive-maintenance approach. The preventive-maintenance approach is far superior to after-the-fact repairs to already seriously impaired employee relations.

We/They: The Invisible Divider

The first step toward maintaining a unionfree and productive environment in your organization is to awaken management awareness of the "we vs. they" assumptions implicit in most management systems. Most managers have been conditioned to think that "we" the management are superior to "they" the laborers. This terminology creates a mind set which establishes an artificial division between employees. It presumes that only managers have the right or the capacity to think and decide. With this right go innumerable privileges, some of the most apparent of which are fancy job titles, better pay, better benefits, stock options, reserved parking and fancy lunches.

Organizations promote a "we vs. they" mind set in both overt and subtle ways that show up in policies, practices and procedures. Although this mind set may not be visible to managers, it certainly is to everybody else—the legions who come to feel like second-class employees.

Much of the we/they mentality is inherent in management history and traditions. Management first became important during the Industrial Revolution. Before then, there were few big institutions. Government was small, companies were small. Only the Catholic Church and the military were historically large. When *management* was created to run the growing industrial organizations, managers looked for a role model and selected the military. The textbook was the officer's manual from the Prussian Army. With the military role model came concepts such as chain of command, officers and enlisted men, authority of command, rights of the haves, and the duties of the have-nots. Transpose that philosophy to today, and it is known as management and labor—a dichotomy ripe for labor unions as a third party.

The we/they mind set currently pervades most organizations. It is so much a part of the corporate culture that even the best-intentioned managers are immersed in it. It is implicit in the pyramid-shaped hierarchial organizational chart. It is reinforced by management training programs and MBA programs that teach a two-class mind set. Managers are taught that their jobs are to plan, organize, delegate, coordinate, control and motivate the "workforce." Policies given to managers assume "we vs. they." *Managers* develop long-range planning budgets and pay systems and assume profit and loss responsibility. *Managers* account for the costs of direct and indirect labor among exempt and nonexempt employees. *Managers* need a special employee relations department because they are too busy doing their jobs—planning, deciding and controlling—to effectively relate to other employees.

This elitist mentality also permeates organizational language. We "manage," they "work"; we "lead," they "follow"; we "think," they "do"; we "talk," they "listen." Managers have "responsibilities," employees have "jobs." Managers are "developed," employees are "trained." Managers form "teams," employees form "workgroups."

Managers benevolently bestow employee cafeterias, employee parking lots, employee handbooks, and employee time clocks. The prefix "employee" is the key. *(Translation: employees use; managers don't.)*

On the other hand, when managers bestow perks upon themselves, "company" is the preferred prefix—think of company planes, company cars, company expense accounts, and company American Express cards. The prefix "company" is also used when managers want to participate in and also take credit for a certain practice, for example, company picnics, company Christmas parties, and company recreational activities.

Sometimes subtle, sometimes not so subtle, dualistic thinking divides an organization into two nouns: management and labor—two distinct things. Such distinctions create a self-fulfilling prophesy, the cumulative effects of

Strategic Approaches to Making Unions Unnecessary

which are overwhelming. If managers view themselves as a first party and workers as a second party, then a gap appears which permits a third party to enter. Few managers consciously or deliberately set out to open the gap. They are simply unaware.

"We vs. They" Checklist

Numerous management behaviors can contribute to a we/they environment. Often managers justify or rationalize these actions, but if other employees believe they create a two-class mind set, they do!

Do you and/or other managers in your organization . . . ? Yes No ?

1. Refer to others as "workers"?
2. Have accounting reports with "direct/indirect labor"?
3. Enter by a separate door from others?
4. Not think of yourselves as "employees"?
5. Sign your full name and title to internal memos?
6. Eat lunch only with other managers?
7. Have coffee served to you in your office?
8. Always "dress for success"?
9. Never place your own phone calls?
10. Hold employee meetings only when scheduled?
11. Rarely come out 2nd or 3rd shift?
12. Handle "open door" cases only by appointment?
13. Hang your diplomas on the wall?
14. Speak only "proper" English and no slang?
15. Go only to the office area or executive restrooms?
16. Always sit at the head of the conference table?
17. Keep employees waiting for meetings?
18. Get faster service on insurance claims?
19. Have offices sized by rank?
20. Have your secretary water your plants?
21. Have personalized stationery and note pads?
22. Have your name on your office door?
23. Walk through the plant without stopping?
24. Introduce visitors only to managers?
25. Keep a copy of the organization chart available?
26. Have company cars?
27. Not know the name of every employee who works for you?
28. Have problem-solving meetings only with "experts"?
29. Never go to employees' funerals?
30. Get paid on different days than others?
31. Not have to show your badge to enter?

Making Unions Unnecessary

	Yes	No	?
32. Have to make an appointment to see your boss?	☐	☐	☐
33. Never walk around just for the sake of walking around?	☐	☐	☐
34. Delegate the giving of service pins?	☐	☐	☐
35. Have different color hard hats than other employees?	☐	☐	☐
36. Blame the government for EEO problems?	☐	☐	☐
37. Try to give the "right impression" to employees?	☐	☐	☐
38. Use a script in employee speeches?	☐	☐	☐
39. Have Christmas parties just for the office group?	☐	☐	☐
40. Always feel you must be "doing something"?	☐	☐	☐
41. Never appear at new employee orientation?	☐	☐	☐
42. Never ask to be shown how to run the equipment?	☐	☐	☐
43. Never stand around the parking lot B.S.'ing?	☐	☐	☐
44. Hold meetings only in your office, not in the shop?	☐	☐	☐
45. Think of budget before people?	☐	☐	☐
46. Use the term "Bullpen"?	☐	☐	☐
47. Get mad when someone takes your parking place?	☐	☐	☐
48. Never do anything spontaneously outrageous?	☐	☐	☐

For all the ones you answered yes, think how your employees may perceive these actions. No one of these behaviors in and of itself creates a two-class mind set; it is the cumulative effects that are overwhelming.

Scorecard

Count Your "Yes" Responses

ZERO to 10 INCIPIENT WE/THEY. Generally exhibited by new MBAs, recent transferees from headquarters, newly promoted managers, VP's relatives and recipients of large pay increases.

11 to 20 MILD WE/THEY. Generally exhibited by second generation owners, graduates of "Dress for Success" seminars, readers of time management books, recent transferees to headquarters, and managers who get lots of calls from recruiters.

21 to 30 CHRONIC WE/THEY. Generally exhibited by ex-military officers below the rank of Colonel, graduates of Ivy League colleges, former football stars, holders of stock options, and members of the corporate job evaluation committee.

31 to 40 HOPELESS WE/THEY. Generally exhibited by persons aspiring to be VPs, instructors in time management, readers of books on "how to increase your word power," managers who fear termination, and anyone who received two promotions in one year.

41 to 50 TERMINAL WE/THEY. Generally exhibited by NLRB members, union busters, holders of company-issued gold American Express cards, people who change companies frequently, and managers with a speaker phone.

We Plus They Is Us

Managers have been taught to plan, organize, delegate, coordinate, control and motivate through front line supervisors. Policies descend from the fourth floor corner office of the Crystal Palace in Emerald City. Supervisors and "supervisees" are excluded from the *process* of designing management systems. They are expected to expertly execute policies and procedures they don't *own* or which are in conflict with their value systems. This is not necessarily bad management; it's simply traditional.

If managers continue this traditional mode, they risk exposing their organizations to third parties. Visualize a gear drive: big wheels connect to medium-sized wheels, which connect to small wheels, which finally connect to little cogs. When the big wheels turn one degree, the little cogs spin wildly. Because there are more cogs than big wheels, through *concerted activity* they can throw a wrench into the system and stop the big wheels cold—and look for the union label on the wrench.

The *process* of creating unionfree and effective employee relations policies is more important than the resulting *content*. The traditional approach is the "big wheels" talk to each other and conjure a policy, or listen to the "Human Resources Director" make a presentation. After approval, the new policy descends upon the local management like Moses' stone tablets and is then relayed to the supervisors. And if the supervisors resist? They get a training program, which is why much of supervisor training consists of teaching smart people to follow insipid policies *they do not own*.

The solution to the "we vs. they" problem, which characterizes many organizations, is simply to create a single "us." View all managers as employees and all employees as managers. As long as managers exclude supervisors and other employees from the *process of gaining ownership*, the we/they syndrome flourishes.

How can local managers and supervisors truly *own* the systems they use to manage if they do not help create them? How can different employee value systems be expressed in design and communication without being a part of the *process*? It is the *process* that changes minds, not the program *content*. No wonder so much resistance to change abounds in the work place!

Here's a "We Plus They Is Us" approach:

1. Set goals for the organization.
2. Share with employees information about methods, constraints and resource limits.
3. Provide the opportunity for employees to become involved and participate in the design of systems and procedures they will use to accomplish the goals for management.

This process is simply the reverse of standard practice. The traditional management approach is backwards. The paradox is that managers do not lose control using this process; they actually gain it. *The belief in some control over one's situation produces persistence in the task.*

A Model of Shared Qualitative Goals

To help you develop your own shared qualitative goals, here is a model that has been used successfully by a major corporation.

We recognize obligations to our shareholders, customers and employees; we strive to balance our responses to their demands, meeting our obligations to each and sacrificing none.

We recognize employees as individuals with different interests, abilities, needs and values. Our goal is to provide them with appropriate compensation, good working conditions and opportunities for personal development and advancement consistent with the individual's ability and desire.

The major factors in selecting new employees will be individual ability and the fit between interests, ability and job requirements. The major factors in promotion will be demonstrated growth and potential for further growth. We strive to eliminate all barriers to equal opportunity.

Employees will be informed about our philosophy, the company and its relation to their jobs; they will have access to the information necessary to perform work effectively.

Systems and procedures will be designed to effect this philosophy; systems and procedures will be open and flexible enough to be influenced by employees at all levels.

Compensation systems are designed to attract and retain competent people, encourage superior performance, provide internal equity, and establish and maintain the company in a competitive position with like industries and within the local working communities.

Benefits structures will be integrated with government programs and designed to protect employees and their families against the financial hazards of ill health, old age and premature death.

We will deal directly with employees. People have the explicit right to speak for themselves, and we believe our personnel philosophy and the attainment of these goals make third party representation unnecessary and undesirable for all employees.

Trust in Management

What affects employee attitudes on trust in management? We recently completed research with clients whose employee attitude scores on "I have confidence in the fairness of management" were either in the top 10 percent or the bottom 10 percent once again confirms that *management visibility* is the key element. In organizations where managers are highly visible and interactive with nonmanagement employees, scores in "confidence in the fairness of management" are high. This "visibility" is *always* face-to-face and carried out in two ways—Open Floor and Open Door. These organizations prominently feature their Open Door philosophy in the company handbooks—it is always near the front, and often on the very first page. In organizations with low scores on this same question, the Open Door policy is either not mentioned or is buried deep in the handbook.

A second fact determined from this recent research is that in organizations with highly favorable employee attitudes, managers regularly meet with nonmanagement employees and hold open-forum style discussions. These meetings are part of the management *philosophy*, are usually described in the handbook as *policy*, and are most definitely *practiced*. In low scoring organizations, either no such practice exists or the meetings are infrequent and almost exclusively one-way speeches rather than discussions. In sum, managers whose employees trust them have high visibility, whether through one-on-one Open Door meetings, walking the floor, or group meetings. Nonmanagement employees clearly understand who and what "management" is.

"Consistency" was another important determinant of trust in management. The feedback meeting notes from employees with highly favorable attitudes *not even once* mentioned the word "inconsistent", but in notes from meetings with unfavorable employee attitudes, the word "inconsistent" was frequently mentioned. When there is a high correlation between what managers *say* they will do and what they actually *do*, they are consistent and have employees who believe in them.

This finding raises the same questions as such inconsistent practices as excused/unexcused attendance policies, imprecise or nonexistent performance standards, and bell-shaped distribution curves for employee performance rankings.

If your company still abides by such archaic management practices as "closed doors" or delays in resolving employee problems, we can guarantee that these practices are eroding employee confidence in the fairness of management. If you still have not implemented a no-fault attendance system or have not tied performance ratings to individual performance standards, you still have enormous reservoirs of inconsistency. The reasons for low morale are crystal clear. There are no surprises in the study results—these results simply confirm what common sense alone should tell every manager.

How can you find out what needs to be changed in your organization? Go ask your people. Get nonmanagement employees together with supervisors and managers in ad hoc committees. Find out what needs to be changed, and then *change it!* And do it now!

If the people in your organization currently have a high level of trust in management, your managers need to keep on doing what they're doing and keep an eye open for further improvement. There is no limit to the depth of trust . . . or the degree of competence.

Pride in the Organization

Trust in management and pride in the organization are closely related issues. In fact, it may be impossible to have one without the other. Most people have a strong desire to have pride in any organization or group with which they are associated. Regardless of whether the group be social, business or religious, most people want to be personally proud of the association and also to have others view the organization favorably. This tendency is so strong that it takes significant levels of inappropriate behavior to cause the majority to lose these feelings. When large numbers of employees lose pride in their company, it is a clear indication—probably more than any other issue—that there are serious employee relations problems.

Employees report that one of the key causes is management behavior that signals a disregard for customer satisfaction. High on the list of such behavior is a low regard for quality standards, such as knowingly shipping questionable products or delivering marginal service because it will probably sneak by. Employees also notice and remember that quality standards appear to be flexible when end-of-month pressures surface or when parts shortages occur and we reinspect to lower tolerances. Large doses of this have been apparent in the U.S. auto industry over the past decade, and numerous customers and employees alike have lost confidence in the product because of a strong belief that dedication to quality was simply a slogan, and the practice was "spit, band-aids and bailing wire." Regardless of the rationale, this behavior will be viewed as dishonest and will ultimately yield attitudes in even the best employees that the organization represents nothing but a paycheck—preferably a big one. If employees must become prostitutes to sales billed at any cost, they will make sure they are high-priced ones.

For the good, caring, qualified employee (which describes the overwhelming majority of the workforce), the existence of and tolerance for shoddy work and poor performance can be a major turn-off. In much the same way that disregard for quality can depress employee attitudes, the continued survival of individuals or groups that do not perform to even minimum performance standards will aggravate employees and may even pull the entire organization down to the lowest common denominator. Employees know who the losers are and cannot be expected to think highly of any organization that tolerates those who are unable or unwilling to do their part; it matters not that the tolerance is based on a misguided belief that a positive employee relations program requires ignoring such failures. A corollary to this that can cause even more widespread unfavorable feelings is hiring or promotion standards that are so low as to be nonexistent. Screening for "warm bodies" or requiring only that applicants be able to read and write (or know someone who can) can never enhance the belief that the organization is special and seeks only the best.

Another factor reported by employees as causing lack of pride in an organization is conduct by management that causes a bad reputation in the community and/or a bad corporate reputation. This occurs when managers, individually or as a group, demonstrate insensitivity to ethical, moral or legal standards and get caught. Public drunkenness, morals charges, and other varieties of uncouth behavior have eroded many managers' reputations and also caused long-term bad feelings for the entire company. More serious are actions which violate local, state or federal law. Serious safety and health problems at the facility; misrepresentations and half-truths to the SEC, shareholders and financial community; and pollution and other environmental abuses are examples of acts that can damage reputations and employees' pride in the organization. The most potent reputation killer is criminal activity such as embezzlement, stock fraud, and the ever-popular numbers manipulation on government contracts. These cause serious long-term problems even when the guilty individual was acting solely out of personal greed. Employees, potential applicants and the general public often believe this is yet another manifestation that company greed and pursuit of profits know no bounds.

All For One Or None For All?

Not only must employees and management trust each other and be able to work together, but also, groups of employees must trust one another and be able to work together. "There is not enough cooperation between my work group and others we work with," is a simple statement with deadly consequences, yet 50 percent of over one-half million employees in CVR's attitude survey data base agree with it. It is consistently among the worst-ranked items on the CVR employee attitude surveys, and among the most difficult to improve.

The amount of time, money, quality, quantity, effort and goodwill lost because of work group cooperation problems has never been measured, but it is most probably staggering.

Some of our research shows that improved communications processes, such as scheduling overlapping meetings for different shifts, holding joint meetings with departments that frequently interact, and a management that "walks the floor" and talks regularly with employees throughout the organization, help encourage cooperation between work groups. The rest of our research, mainly in the form of actual attitude survey feedback notes from a range of organizations, shows that some of the most frustrating and debilitating work group cooperation problems *cannot be solved by the workgroups themselves.*

One of the biggest problems for manufacturing companies is the month-end billing cycle. Here is the scenario: Accounting systems for cost accounting and inventory call for monthly billings. Top management, eager to show progressive monthly and quarterly billings and meet ambitious forecasts, pressures the sales force (which generally works on some kind of a commission basis) to get those orders in by the monthly deadline. Orders flood in during the five working days before the deadline, and *of course* most are guaranteed to be shipped within a certain time frame.

Meanwhile, back at the plant, the purchasing, production scheduling, and various manufacturing departments are constantly under the gun to keep work-in-process (WIP) to a minimum and to keep inventory low. The stores and shipping departments, too, are constantly under the gun to keep order fill high and order turnaround time low.

Suddenly, a huge pile of orders comes in and everyone is thrown into chaos.

The production scheduling department is upset with purchasing because there aren't enough component parts on hand, and sub-assembly runs out of parts. Final assembly doesn't have anything to do because WIP inventory is so low there aren't enough parts to keep everyone busy, and since there aren't enough component parts for sub-assembly, both departments sit around waiting for purchasing to expedite component parts from vendors. Of course the vendors charge extra for "rush" orders, so the cost forecast is blown and the cost per item rises. To get final assembly moving, the people in sub-assembly have to work overtime. This drives the cost per item up further. In addition, sales is upset with shipping because customers are complaining their orders haven't been shipped or are incomplete; shipping is upset with stores because there aren't enough parts in inventory and backorders are building up; stores is frustrated because final assembly isn't producing any parts; final assembly is impatiently waiting on sub-assembly which is waiting on purchasing which is pleading with vendors. Throughout the entire process, everyone wants to know why production scheduling didn't anticipate the problem.

Granted, this scenario is the extreme, but most organizations, whether product- or service-oriented, have one or more of these problems. Instead of a heavy domino effect, it may be only a few departments—workflow systems may be designed so that departments work well independently but can't function smoothly when they have to interact.

Also, the more levels of management an organization has, the less likely people are to believe that their problems will be solved. Many frustrated employees believe upward communication gets caught in a "bottleneck" and seldom reaches the manager who needs to hear it.

Is it fair to expect people to have good attitudes about work group cooperation when the very system they must work within destines them to constant problems and fire-fighting? Is it fair to tell people, "you need to cooperate more with your co-workers," when they have little or no chance of changing the system? Or is it time management devoted some heavy-duty time and energy to unearthing and solving the problems that predetermine work-group friction.

Summary and Key Points

Even the best of strategies do not always work as they were intended. We should recognize that even in the best of organizations, union organizing drives will sometimes occur. This does not mean that there is necessarily a problem within the organization, because organizing drives may occur for a number of reasons. There are malcontents and troublemakers in any organization who may want to try to bring in a union because of their negative feelings toward management. Moreover, the actions of one or two supervisors, contrary to policy and without the knowledge of top management, can cause incidents that encourage workers to turn to a union for help.

Organizing drives seldom, if ever, come from outside the organization. Regardless of how intensive the external organizing drive may appear, it cannot be successful without the support of employees on the inside. The experience of many unionfree companies as well as those that have become organized is that most campaigns actually start on the inside of the company, and union sympathizers later seek outside support and affiliation from professional organizers.

Taking actions to undermine the union's strength after an organizing drive starts, by making changes and improvements in the way people are dealt with, may destroy the "laboratory conditions" under which the National Labor Relations Board (NLRB) requires that a union election be held. Therefore, the old saying that "an ounce of prevention is worth a pound of cure" certainly holds true when dealing with employees and union organizing drives. Perhaps more important, though somewhat more subtle, the sudden interest in employee welfare and attitudes after a union shows up at the door is often seen as proof positive that management cares little about its employees. It disregards them until a union shows up, then proceeds to make repairs to employee relations. This is the "jelly bean theory" described previously.

Corporations that get a union deserve it, and they deserve the kind they get. Self-audit 3 in Appendix A can help you find out whether your company "deserves" a union, and to see where you stand on the road from "we vs. they" to "us."

Seven personnel areas are the keys to maintaining unionfree status. They are employee attitudes and value systems, job design, management systems and procedures, growth opportunity and advancement, pay and benefits, equal employment opportunity and facilities and working conditions. For each of these key personnel areas there is a strategic approach that is likely to serve the purpose of making unions unnecessary. These strategic approaches not only achieve the goal of productivity but also maintain morale so that employees will not feel the need to engage in concerted protective activity.

CHAPTER 6

EMPLOYEE ATTITUDES

The first of the strategic areas is employee attitudes, which depend in large measure on communication and persuasion which, in turn, depend on credibility. We have already discussed the necessity of the organization having a clear policy statement on operating unionfree. However, "actions speak louder than words"; what we do and what we say in management must be consistent. There is no credibility in initiating employee communications after an organizing drive has started. Rather, it is day-in, day-out communication upward, downward, and laterally throughout the organization well in advance of a union organizing drive that is the key to success. It has been stated this way; "When in doubt, tell the truth." Credibility is established only by being credible; that is, there must be a high correlation between what we say and what we do.

Psychological research provides a great deal of material on communication and persuasion that has direct application to maintaining unionfree status. In the area of persuasion of human beings and how opinions and attitudes are changed, there are several well-understood phenomena.

The first of these is how to present the issues. Although in some circumstances a mild fear appeal, a threat, is persuasive, in general, it is inappropriate to create fear in the minds of employees regarding what might happen if a union were to be formed. There will also be more opinion change in the direction management wants if you state the conclusions explicitly than if you let the audience draw their own conclusions. For example, management should present a strong case for why it is more beneficial to the employees not to have a union than it is to have one. You can allude to the fact that unions have sometimes helped people as well as corporations, but then stress the conclusion that unions are not necessary in your particular company.

In addition, the impact of a persuasive appeal is enhanced by requiring active rather than passive participation by the listener. Getting the audience to respond with a show of hands to questions—"Did the union get you your job?" "Can a union keep your job?" "Has a union gotten you the pay increases that you've had in the past?"—will persuade more people to the management position than simply speaking to them without any audience response and participation. The exception to this general principle is during the last moments of a union campaign just prior to election, when presenting your side of the argument forceably will strongly influence employees to vote "no" to the union question.

You should recognize that for every appeal you offer, the union is offering other appeals. You can significantly undercut the force of a union argument by presenting both sides and answering the objections and questions well in advance of the union's communications. Arguments presented at the beginning or at the end of the communication will be remembered better than the arguments presented in the middle. Therefore, management should present its case first, give the union side in the middle, then draw its conclusions at the end, thus creating a more indelible image in the minds of employees. Facts and information alone almost never change attitudes. It is necessary to draw conclusions and state the position that you wish people to follow. While humor is sometimes appropriate, unionization has such an impact on employees' lives and particularly their life at work that it should be used very cautiously and very mildly.

Employee opinions and attitudes are strongly influenced by the groups to which they belong or want to belong. If they already have an affinity for the union, or if some of their associates within the organization are actively campaigning on behalf of the union, they will be significantly influenced. However, the supervisor is a significant person in the everyday working life of an individual employee, and good supervisory contact and communication can offset the appeals of unions, whether they're made by peer groups or by external organizers.

Opinions that people make known to others are harder to change than opinions that they hold privately. Therefore, active union organizers who are vocal in their anti-company statements will rarely change their position once they have gone on public record.

The changes of opinion that follow appeals are not always consistent and persistent. In time, the effects of a persuasive communication tend to wear off. Because of this, the organization must state its position about unions from time to time. For example, the employees should be reminded of the company's position on unions at least once a year, and certainly in the beginning stages of an organizing drive. Research on opinion change indicates that change is more persistent over a period of time if the persuasive appeal is repeated. Since the supervisor is essential to the maintenance of unionfree status as well as to productivity, supervisors certainly must be in the audience. It is necessary for top management to influence not only hourly and salaried employees, but their supervision first and foremost.

Research has shown that different kinds of people react differently to persuasion: personality traits affect susceptibility to persuasion. More will be said later about this research on employees' reaction to unions in relation to their personality traits and value systems.

Who does the persuading has a significant impact. There is more opinion change in the desired direction for a communicator with high credibility than for one with low credibility. For example, a plant manager who is notorious for not living up to his word will not be able to influence very many employees in the direction desirable to the company, because his actions have belied his words. Many unionfree organizations have found that the immediate supervisor has a higher credibility than top management, particularly when the first time that top management speaks to the employees is after an organizing drive has started. Since people are persuaded more effectively by a communicator they perceive to be similar to themselves, much of the communication about unions needs to come through the immediate supervisor, who is closer in many ways to the workforce than an executive.

Management should not be reluctant to ask for an extreme opinion change, for often, the more extreme the position change asked for, the more actual shift in attitudes occurs. But remember that sensationalism is among the least effective forms of persuasion in producing long-term attitude change. Management should be cautious about using the extreme emotional appeals that are often found in the motion picture films available, which overdramatize the plight of people during union strife.

Attitude Surveys

Getting people to listen is probably the foremost problem in management. We often send messages out through the organization with the assumption that everybody is listening and understanding in exactly the way intended. Many managers presume that their communiques are reaching and penetrating the minds of their employees, but they never bother to check. In reality, in human communications, there is often a serious gap between the message that was sent and the one received. The amount of time and money spent on communications directed from management to the employees usually exceeds tenfold the amount spent on listening to people and getting feedback about the effectiveness of the management process as perceived by the members of the organization.

Some organizations have made extensive use of employee attitude surveys to bridge the communications gap between management and labor. In addition, they may provide grievance procedures, open-door policies, rap sessions, and interviews in an attempt to find out how people feel about what the corporation is doing. Other top managers simply assume they know how people feel because they are receiving reports from managers down the chain. As most studies of human communication show, the degree of filtering and distortion that occurs (particularly when hierarchy is involved) can block effective upward feedback or distort it to the degree that the situation is perceived as positive when, in fact, there is a great deal of unrest among the employees.

Attitude surveys can help improve management credibility. They can also raise a manager's level of understanding about how people really feel, provided employees are given an opportunity to address management in a candid fashion. Without upward communication bypassing the chain of command, there is no way for management to know exactly people's candid and undistorted feelings. For example, in one case an attitude survey predicted a great deal of employee unrest, and interest in forming a labor union. The survey was disbelieved by top management because, in interrogating middle management and supervision, they found few problems. Follow-up interviews with employees and supervisors also showed very little employee discontent and dissatisfaction. However, a few months later, a labor union filed a petition for recognition and was able to show that more than 30 percent of the employees had signed union cards. Evidently, there was a significant gap, and distortion occurred as information was passed up the line.

Hierarchies have a tendency to filter bad news on the way up and bring forward only information that middle management believes is most acceptable to top management. Some of this distortion is inadvertent, but some of it is blatantly self-serving. Some human resources departments also accommodate the desires of top management and tend to discredit or discount evidence of poor morale. In some organizations, significant employee dissatisfaction has been hidden from the view of top management with the hope that it will go away on its own or that, with a delay, the problem may be resolved and eliminated before key executives have to get involved. Given these forms of organization behavior, how can corporations and top management design a system of upward communication that automatically corrects for these tendencies?

Attitude surveys are increasingly utilized by unionfree companies that wish to remain that way. It is our experience, however, that many executives are reluctant to engage in attitude surveying because of a myriad of technical questions about how to get started and what to do with the data once it is collected. The purpose of this section is to answer these questions and provide guidance in the implementation and utilization of attitude surveys. These views are based on years of practical experience in creating and applying attitude surveys in a number of organizations. It is not our purpose to engage in theoretical discussions of attitude measurement and scaling techniques or, for that matter, complicated statistics, but rather to present straight answers to the questions managers most frequently ask.

1. *Why do a formal survey?*
   There are many ways to assess employee attitudes. You can look at turnover, examine your history of union activity, measure productivity and quality, listen to the grapevine, read the comments on the restroom walls or talk to a few people. All these methods will provide some data; however, without valid statistics and standardized comparative items, you'll never be sure whether your data is sound.

2. *What is the value of a survey if everyone is happy?*
   In the first place, how do you know everyone is happy? In the second place, assuming you are right, organizations with relatively favorable attitudes use surveys to make sure attitudes stay that way.

3. *Are employee attitudes important in and of themselves?*
   Our view is that they are important, regardless of any impact attitudes may have on productivity or quality. It is also our belief that

positive attitudes can and do improve overall performance.

4. *Aren't attitudes just perceptions and not representative of "reality"?*

Attitudes represent the reality of the work world as each employee perceives it. Employees' perceptions are their reality. To question the validity of their feelings is fruitless. Managers need to view the survey through the eyes of employees and not attempt to reinterpret the results according to management's "reality."

5. *Won't a survey be a threat to some managers?*

Good managers are never threatened by an attitude survey, because they view it as an opportunity to achieve excellence. Poor managers are threatened not only by an attitude survey but by anything that may expose their incompetence.

6. *Can an employee attitude survey open up a "can of worms"?*

We certainly hope so, if you have one! Because if *you* don't open it up, some third party will be happy to provide that service for you.

7. *Are there times when an employee attitude survey should not be considered?*

There are times when it may be best not to conduct a survey: during an organizing drive, during holidays, right after a change in pay and benefits, in the midst of an organization restructuring, after drastic budget cuts, or when you lack management commitment to follow through.

8. *Does our past experience with surveys have any bearing on doing one now?*

It is irrelevant whether a survey was done in the past. If you did one and it was unsuccessful, you may have either used the wrong survey or not followed through. If you haven't done one, start now.

9. *But aren't attitudes relative?*

Definitely. That's why statistics are important. A reliable statistical data base lets you compare relative attitudes within your organization and to other organizations. You can also make meaningful comparisons among demographic groups—whites/blacks, males/females, short/long service, etc. Most important are your survey results compared to your own standards of excellence.

10. *What kind of program seems to work best?*

Some programs are designed exclusively for management use and analysis, with the focus on coming up with the right answers. Others provide a "process" that involves all employees in problem solving and goal setting and that focuses on coming up with the right *questions.*

11. *What do you mean by "process" versus "program"?*

A program has a start and a finish. A process is continuous. A program is generally a short-term project for solving a specific problem. A process is meant to embed itself in the mainstream of operations. A program is imposed from outside; your employees don't own it. An employee relations process is psychologically owned by employees.

Conducting the survey is merely the first step in an ongoing process. It must be viewed as a means, not an end. That is, the main purpose of the survey is to identify strengths and weaknesses and to serve as a means of opening communications among all employees, who then can help in solving problems and implementing positive change.

12. *How many questions should be asked?*

Most corporations can cover their employee morale territory with approximately twenty questions. Usually this gives sufficient data, and going beyond this often results in more data than can be handled. If too many questions are asked, the statistical manipulation of the data often gets in the way of the problem-solving activities. Further, there is no need to consume a great deal of time filling out a questionnaire on subjects that are of lesser importance. The key, then, is to select the twenty areas that need to be sampled and in which improvements can result, and to write the statements in language that can be easily read and understood by nearly all employees. We recommend that the twenty statements deal with the following issues:

1. The work itself
2. Workgroup cooperation
3. Advancement opportunities
4. Working conditions
5. Performance feedback
6. Confidence in management
7. Retirement plan
8. Job security
9. Rules and procedures
10. Job freedom
11. Supervision
12. Company pride
13. Fairness of pay
14. Seeking outside jobs
15. Favoritism
16. Use of abilities
17. Job future
18. Changes in company overall
19. Job expectations
20. Insurance benefits

13. *Don't we need different questions for professionals?*

Our research proves conclusively that it is unnecessary. The same issues are important to all segments of the workforce.

14. *Should we survey the entire organization at one time?*

Yes, if at all possible; however, sometimes it's just not practical or even logistically possible. Basically, survey as many employees as you

Employee Attitudes

can comfortably handle at one time and what suits your organizational structure and style. It doesn't make much difference which way you do it, as long as it's all done eventually. Once the survey process is started in one part of an organization, the employees who were not included expect to someday be involved.

15. *Is a survey also an audit of managers?*

Yes. For example, most people get a physical checkup each year even when they are feeling well, hoping to either uncover any problems or to confirm that none exists. If we do have problems, it gives us a chance to remedy them before they become life threatening.

We can adopt the same concept and process to manage employee attitudes. A survey can reveal favorable attitudes which you want to maintain and, at the same time, uncover problems in time for them to be resolved.

Some companies incorporate survey data into their MBO process and managerial performance reviews. These organizations hold managers accountable for the effective use of both physical assets and employees.

16. *Why do companies decide to do a survey?*

Some do it out of fear of a labor union—a "reactive" mode. Most, however, survey for "proactive" reasons. They don't have the old management versus labor mentality; they actually care about what their employees think and feel.

17. *Do employees in better-managed organizations have better attitudes?*

Where favorable employee attitudes are found, better productivity, fewer problems and better quality work are also found. In other words, the expression of employee attitudes is an alternate way of looking at how well the organization works, because an organization is to a large extent the employees. It is easy to buy machinery, buildings and other physical assets. The true test of management is determined by how well those assets are used by people working together to achieve organizational goals.

18. *What if an organization is already unionized?*

That is irrelevant. Employees still have attitudes that are management's responsibility, not the union's. If you are concerned about the attitudes of all employees, whether they have union representation or not, then perhaps you can make all third parties, including unions, unnecessary.

19. *Who should be surveyed?*

Everyone—managers, supervisors, office staff, professionals, production and maintenance employees—even vice-presidents. If the survey is thought to be only for "them" out there in the organization and "we" are not included, that sends a message. Further, if managers have an attitude problem, you will get nowhere until they get their act together. Perhaps the most important reason to include everyone is that

20. *Is a repeat survey necessary? If so, how often should it be conducted?*

   In some ways it is more important than the initial survey. An initial survey gives you a starting point, but the repeat surveys indicate the direction in which attitudes are moving. In other words, although it's important to know where you stand right now, it's even more important to know where you're going and how you're going to get there. Later, measure whether you moved in the right direction. Some companies survey once every 12 months, while others survey once every 24 months. If there is a typical time frame, it is once every 12 to 15 months.

21. *When the results are in, what next?*

   Now the process really begins. Managers and supervisors review the reports, and then the results are fed back to the rest of the employees.

22. *What results should go back to the employees and how should this be done?*

   Each survey group should receive both its individual data and the results for the total organization. These results may also be compared to the company's own internal norms or to national norms.

   Generally, the immediate supervisor of each survey group holds a feedback meeting to report and discuss the survey results. Feedback meetings should occur as quickly as possible. These are the goals of the feedback meetings:

   - Find out what's okay and why (so you can keep it that way).
   - Find out what's so-so and why (so you can make it better).
   - Find out what's not okay and why (so you can change and fix it).

   The initial feedback meeting generally runs two hours. You may shorten the time if you arrange *ad hoc* committees to handle problem-solving special projects outside the regular meetings.

   Keep in mind that this is not a quick fix process. Problems that have accumulated over years cannot be dismissed quickly. Some groups may have a lot of venting during initial sessions.

23. *What if supervisors can't handle a feedback meeting?*

   Most supervisors can handle it with a little preparation. Training materials such as videotapes and printed materials to aid supervisors are available. You will always find a few supervisors, however, who are not qualified to lead such a meeting. In these cases, a member of management or human resources can assist, but competent supervision is the goal.

24. *What should be done with a manager whose results are well below the norms?*

    First, work with that manager to make him or her aware of how attitudes affect organizational performance. Second, get that manager to set a goal and commit to raising attitudes by next year. If that doesn't work, termination may be necessary.

25. *Isn't it management's role to solve problems?*

    Only in the traditional concept of management. Many corporations have found that employees not only have questions, they often have the answers as well. In fact, perhaps 60 percent of problems raised during feedback sessions are solved by the workgroup itself.

26. *Doesn't this whole process take people off the job for a long time?*

    If you consider all employees' jobs to include making positive suggestions and helping to solve problems, then they're still doing their jobs.

27. *How much impact can employee involvement in problem solving really have?*

    Employee involvement can form the basis for continuing dialogue between management and other employees so that problems can be averted before they develop into major issues. It also serves as a vehicle to provide management with continuing, unfiltered, upward feedback.

28. *Are there any criteria we can use to help us choose—or design—an effective and efficient employee attitudes survey?*

    We strongly suggest the following criteria:

    Survey Versatility. The survey process should be designed for use with any employee population.

    Maximum Feasible Simplicity. The survey questionnaire should be short, simply written, values free, yet scientifically developed.

    Predictability. The results should predict vulnerability to unionization and other industrial relations problems.

    Reliance On Outsiders. The survey process should be designed to permit any organization to conduct the survey with minimum reliance on outside consultants.

    Quick Turnaround Time. The survey process should be computerized to ensure quick turnaround and accuracy of results.

    Understandability Of Results. The survey output reports should be designed so all employees are able to quickly and easily understand the results.

    Cost Effectiveness. The survey process should be cost effective.

In summary, attitude surveys can improve the effectiveness of management and provide a significant upward channel for unadulterated, unfiltered feedback. The involvement of managers in the design of the survey system as well as the attitudes to be surveyed is critical. Without key manager involvement, opinion surveys will be a meaningless exercise that will simply raise the frustration level and drive attitudes and morale downward when there is no response following the survey. Downward communication is generally effected easily by management—or, at least, managers believe that this is so. The only way to know whether communications are effective is to close the loop and bring unfiltered upward feedback directly from employees to key managers so that they may measure the impact they are having and the effectiveness of their communications efforts. Attitude measurement is not a new tool, just one that is not applied as often—or as well—as it could be.

Attitude Survey Results. "Work group cooperation," "enough information on how we're doing," and "confidence in the fairness of management" are typically among the lowest-scoring items on the attitude survey. For a list of items that were mentioned by employees as reasons for their negative responses, see Appendix C.

The Power of Group Meetings

One-to-one communications between the supervisor and the person supervised is not only inefficient, it fails to give recognition to the fact that the behavior of groups is much more predictable than the behavior of individuals. A significant number of unionfree companies require by policy that departments or other organizational units hold group meetings at least four times a year. These meetings may cover the status of the business, the competition, new developments, changes in policies and practices, or reiteration of key human resources programs. They also provide an opportunity to restate in short form the company's position on not having a union. Furthermore, they establish the credibility of top managers who appear at the meetings, and supplement the messages being communicated by the supervisors. There should be no surprises for the supervisors at these meetings; they should be briefed in advance and their advice and counsel taken into consideration when the content of the meeting is being established. This also develops a pattern, should the time come when certain messages need to be communicated because an organizing drive is in process or a union election has been scheduled. As a number of studies in organizational behavior have shown, the ability of the individual to relate to the objectives of the organization can be a key factor in productivity. Meetings of this kind are also effective in the maintenance of unionfree status.

Following a departmental meeting, ad hoc committees may be developed to devise and make recommendations on improvements and changes in human resources programs and the operation of the office or factory. In the establishment of ad hoc committees as a follow-on to group meetings, the most conservative approach is for management to select the members, place a member of management or supervision in charge of the meeting, and limit the subject matter to those things for which the committee was established. Some organizations go further, however, and permit employees to select their own representatives. As long as the material developed from the meeting is understood to be an advisement rather than a demand, the possibilities of creating a *de facto* union are minimized. The use of departmental meetings also establishes a pattern for supervisors to emulate on a day-in, day-out basis.

Problem-Solving Orientation

Communications in the unionfree company must take a problem-solving orientation, rather than the approach of who did what to whom and why, which often results in punitive measures. Since communications among human beings is a continuous process, there are innumerable opportunities for miscommunication and misperception to occur. When problems do arise, the objective is to solve the problem rather than to find out who is responsible and take a negative response. The problem-solving orientation enhances management's credibility and gives credence to the concept that the organization is one unit, without the credibility or policy gap between management and labor that unions thrive on. The problem-solving orientation is an attitude of management which, if followed consistently, can permeate the organization so that it becomes legitimate to air difficulties and problems because it is known that the response will be in the direction of resolution rather than punishment.

Open Door

One thing that unions do guarantee to their membership is due process in the resolution of grievances. The majority of unionfree organizations that have maintained that position over the years have used the "open door" approach rather than the step grievance procedure. A union can provide due process in grievances and disputes to the point of reaching the level of upper management with arbitration and conciliation. The rules of this particular game are defined strictly by the contract, and the process operates in a quasi-legal manner. Unionfree organizations are more likely to follow the open-door process, which is looser in its structure and more open to employees pursuing resolution of their grievances with their superiors, the human resources department, or higher management—and not necessarily in that order. Unionized companies' employees have a right under the contract to carry their grievances through a chain of review and appeal. In unionfree companies, this approach seldom works well; in fact, a comparison of a large number of union and unionfree companies shows that even though unionfree companies often have the formalistic approach to grievance handling, it is seldom used. When offered the choice between the formal written grievance procedure and the open-door approach, the vast majority of employees prefer to follow the open-door approach. It is simpler, more efficient, and often results in a more rapid resolution of the issue.

As with every human and organizational process, of course, there are problems involved. Virtually all *unionfree* organizations use, or claim to use, an open-door policy for dealing with employee complaints. The fundamental concept is that an employee should be able to see someone *within* the system so that he or she is not forced to go *outside* the organization. There is little controversy on this aspect of the policy. However, managers still dispute whether an individual should have direct access to whomever he or she wishes to see, or be required to follow the "chain-of-command." Furthermore, in some companies that profess to have an open-door policy, the door really is not open, or in some cases there are two doors—the front one and the back one. Count on the back one being readily available to those who have the audacity to bring their complaints forward. It is necessary to protect individuals with complaints and follow up later to see that they are not being punished for bringing forth their problems.

Although nearly all unionfree institutions have an open-door policy, only about one-half permit and encourage direct access to higher level managers. The other half follow the linear unionized grievance procedure of first discussing the problem with the first-line supervisor, then Human Resources, then step-by-step up the management ladder. Which is preferable?

If the goal is to resolve employee complaints equitably and rapidly using the least time and energy, then direct access to whoever is in the best position to solve the problem is the preferred system. If the objective is to assuage the self-importance of supervisors and mid-level managers, the linear approach is more appropriate. Which approach is better for an organization depends on its particular underlying philosophy.

Management must decide which is more highly valued—solving employee problems or upholding the chain of command. If solving people's problems is more important, then direct access is the only way to go. If following the chain of command is, then have people take a number and form a queue. The more open-minded a management team is, the more likely the direct access method will prevail. The slow, sequential, union-like climb up the management chain is usually evidence of close-mindedness.

Some managers fear that direct access to management will flood the "front office" with malcontent employees. In organizations with competent, confident managers who believe in and support an open-door policy, this simply does not happen. And even if it were to happen, which would you rather have—a lobby full of unhappy employees or a lobby full of happy union organizers? Some managers also fear that intermediate levels of supervision and management are undermined when dissatisfied people "go over their heads." The question to ask here is why do people feel they have to bypass immediate and intermediate management in order to resolve a problem? *Of course* it is always preferable to have an employee initially discuss a complaint with his or her supervisor—but if there truly are open minds behind the open doors, the supervisor need not be the first contact.

One of the key factors in the effective use of the open-door policy is the "24-hour turnaround." Under this concept, employees who have problems may contact any member of management who they feel can help them with their problem. If that problem is something that could have been resolved by their supervisor, they are asked to see their supervisor first and then return if they are still dissatisfied with the response. In any case, they are assured of receiving a response within 24 hours. The 24-hour turnaround is a far better grievance-handling service than unions can provide.

Utilization of the open-door policy sometimes does lead to complaints from supervisors that their authority is being usurped. However, if a company wishes to maintain unionfree status, supervisors must recognize that they have a responsibility to solve problems and that, if they are unable to do so, the employee does have the right to appeal to higher management. If we do not provide such an outlet and a resolution for real or imagined complaints, it is natural for employees to turn to unions, which do have the power to bring a grievance to a resolution.

The open-door policy in the majority of unionfree companies is quite flexible and has very few formal procedures attached to it. People are encouraged to use the open-door system, and although the majority of the complaints are relatively trivial in nature, they are important in the minds of the individuals making the complaint. It is not up to management to judge whether the issue is real or imagined, significant or insignificant; if the individual brings it forward, it is clearly significant in his or her own mind.

The majority of employee complaints involve miscommunication between the individual and the supervisor. Many of these can be resolved expeditiously, at very low cost and at very rapid response time. In the majority of cases, the supervisor's judgment was right. What the employee really wants to know is, can the supervisor make that decision and does the supervisor have the right to talk to him that way? Too often, although the supervisor's judgment was correct, he or she has exhibited a lack of finesse, an arbitrary way of dealing with the situation, and abruptness in communication.

In one case, for example, eight employees approached the human resources director with the complaint that their supervisor had told them that they had to work on Saturday. After much discussion, the real issue came to light: "Can our supervisor make us work overtime on Saturday?" The answer was, "Yes, he can—but when did he tell you that you had to do this?" The employees replied, "He told us a half hour ago, and here it is Friday afternoon and we have plans for the weekend." When told that the supervisor could require them to work overtime, they were satisfied that the supervisor was correct in his judgment but still concerned that he had told them at such a late date. It was necessary to intervene with the supervisor and tell him that he was correct in his judgment but that he should make it a point to notify people of the requirement to work overtime no later than Wednesday afternoon, and if circumstances require that he do it on Friday, then do the human thing and apologize for the lateness of his decision.

The use of the open-door policy and the 24-hour turnaround concept gives much better service in problem resolution than unions can provide. Generally, union grievances take not 24 hours but more like 24 days or longer to reach a resolution, because they involve a lot of legalistic maneuvers and documentation that simply delay the resolution of the issue and create backlogs. Here again, the fundamental tenets of communication apply: credibility and responsiveness.

An open mind is the success ingredient of an open-door policy, but alas, there is no procedure for an open mind. How "open" minds are depends on the *integrity* of the supervisors and managers and whether they put fairness ahead of their own egos. This amazing but true story exemplifies the kind of attitude that makes an open-door policy successful:

> The phone rang in the company president's office, and a staff assistant answered. The voice on the other end said, "I've just been told I've been fired, and I think it is unfair. I want to find out if this open door stuff really works. I want to talk to the president." The staff assistant said, "Hold on a moment," and called the president on his car telephone and repeated what the employee said. The president said, "Tell the man I will see him in my office in two hours, and call the security analysts and tell them I have canceled my speech because I have something more important to do."

Any question as to why this company has never had a union election? Or why they lead their industry in customer service? Or why they have a reputation for excellence in management? We will not tell you the company's name, but we will give you this hint—its initials are IBM.

Suggestion Systems

Employee suggestion systems, with or without financial awards, have been tried by many organizations to improve communications, morale, and productivity. In general, they have been found to be relatively ineffective because the majority of people have their suggestions rejected—they are, in effect, punished for bringing forth ideas for improvement. It is more effective in the long run to incorporate problem-solving techniques for obtaining ideas for improvement and greater productivity into the course of the everyday work, rather than establishing a separate system. However, if you prefer to have a suggestion system, the basic concept is, run it efficiently and do it well; otherwise you will get more problems from employee unrest than benefits from the suggestions.

The Use of Ad Hoc Committees

One device that has proven extremely valuable in improving communications is the use of ad hoc committees. An ad hoc committee is a group of employees selected by management who are charged with examining a problem and coming up with recommendations for solutions. Ad hoc problem-solving committees can be extremely useful means for improving productivity, changing policies and procedures, modifying benefit programs, and obtaining feedback to management on what employees are really concerned about. It is not necessary to have a large committee; twelve people is usually sufficient. They can be set up to operate as a unit for as long as the problem continues and until they reach a resolution. Most organizations that use ad hoc committees change the membership of the committees periodically by replacing one or two members at a time so that there is both continuity and change, rather than having a standing committee that may become a union substitute or a union in fact. It is important that there be no *quid pro quo* involved. Management must maintain control of the committee and be prepared to implement changes without requesting something in return. If management says, "I will give you this if you will give me that," it may create a *de facto* union, and the process of election may be bypassed.

As long as management selects the members, determines how long they will serve, and makes no bargains with the committee, this technique can be an extremely effective way of getting employees involved in eliminating the win-lose, we-they atmosphere between management and labor that makes an organization ripe for unionization. Furthermore, as many organizations have found, there is a great potential for cost effectiveness and productivity improvement in the use of ad hoc committees when they are directed toward solving problems of productivity and work performance.

The function of the committee is advisory; management wants information and advice and will take the recommendations under serious consideration. If there are constraints under which the committee will operate, they should be stated in advance. The function of the committee is to provide information and ideas, and when its function is served, the committee should be disbanded until the next opportunity to utilize an ad hoc committee arises.

A brief example will indicate the contribution that ad hoc committees can make. In one company, the personnel department devised a new performance appraisal program, including forms, procedures, and handbooks. This was sent throughout the organization for supervisors to use with hourly people in assembly operations. It was met with indifference and hostility on the part of both the supervisors and the people they supervised. The prime reason for the problem was that the systems and procedures that had been designed would be appropriate to use with professionals, but not for people in production jobs. Management's reaction was to engage all the people concerned in an extensive training program and teach them how to use the system, but it became evident early that the problem was not a misunderstanding of the system but the inappropriateness of its design. Rather than force the system on the people, therefore, management gave supervisors and their workers the opportunity to redesign the system according to the kinds of jobs and people involved. There were design limitations: personality traits were not to be used, and the system was to be quantitative to the greatest extent possible. As a result, several ad hoc committees were able to design a new system that both met the needs and purposes of the people on the line and suited management's objective of evaluating performance. The new system, once installed, was easily operated, because it was designed according to the needs of the people that utilized it rather than by the theories of the "experts."

A major advantage of ad hoc committees is that they create resident peer group experts whose credibility with the employees is going to be far greater than management's. The committee members also have a personal involvement in and commitment to the solutions that come out of the committee. They know exactly why things are the way they are instead of some other way, because they were there. They can be very powerful communicators and opinion leaders. The credibility of management, in other words, may be established indirectly through the utilization of ad hoc committees.

In a few unionfree organizations, the use of committees has reached the point that no human resources policy in the company will be changed without the prior involvement of the people. In one company, the president of the organization will make no changes in human resources policies and programs unless the employees and the supervisors have first been consulted, not to vote, but simply to listen and ask questions. It is a form of market research, using employees instead of customers. In this way, the needs, aspirations and value systems of the employees are taken into account through the use of the process called "involvement." For some ideas on how to increase involvement, see Appendix D.

Written Communications

By their very nature, written communications are one-way communications from management to the employees, with little opportunity for feedback, but if used in conjunction with meetings, attitude surveys, and ad hoc committees, they can be useful means of presenting management's message.

Handbook. The employee handbook is a common form of written communication. Employee handbooks, however, have often been written in the language and terminology of the human resources department, or even worse—legalese. Not only are they too long and wordy, but they are too complicated in their attempts to explain highly complex subjects. Because of the differences among people, in terms of their personalities, values and the language they use to communicate, most employee handbooks cannot be relied on as meaningful tools for management communication to employees. They are, in fact, not read by the majority of the employees. When they have a problem, most people go to the human resources department or to their supervisor and ask a question and hope to get an answer.

One organization found that most of their employees read comic books, and a large number of them read *only* comic books. Consequently, their employee handbook takes the form of a 16-page color cartoon comic book to explain, in a simple manner, such subjects as pensions, profit sharing, insurance, work rules, attendance procedures, and time clocks. This has been met with a positive response from a majority of employees, who find that this is something that they can understand, whereas the typical employee handbook is beyond the comprehension of everyone except the individual who wrote it in the first place.

This is not to say that handbooks cannot be a valuable adjunct to employee communications; it is simply that in a majority of cases, they have been written for the human resources department rather than for the intended audience. A few organizations have established ad hoc committees of employees to help design and write the employee handbook or to act as an editorial review board, not to create policy, but to see that the content is meaningful to the intended audience.

In today's litigious environment, attorneys often advise the inclusion of "employment-at-will," "not a contract," and "can be changed at management's discretion." These statements, albeit protective, are negative and are threatening to many employees. The solution? Put them on a page of their own, to be signed and dated by the employee to verify that the message was received. The page can then be removed from the handbook and filed elsewhere.

Communications Media

A number of companies have depended heavily on employee newspapers in the belief that people will read whatever is printed, particularly if it comes from management. More than one study has shown, however, that employee newspapers suffer from some of the same ills as employee handbooks. The term "employee newspaper" is often a misnomer, particularly with regard to the parts of the newspaper that are concerned with the economic facts of the business. The things relating to employee recreation and human interest may be followed closely or to some degree; the announcement of an improved benefit program, provided it is described in terms of the benefits and not the techniques, will be read and comprehended by employees. But financial matters are another story. One of the most notorious examples of poor communication was the printing of a great deal of financial data from one corporation's annual report on the front page of the employee newspaper with the belief that the employees would read it. A follow-up study showed that only 15 percent of the employees read and understood it—and all of them were members of management. We have here a clear case of the typical problem of management talking to itself and believing that other employees are listening and comprehending.

Self-Audit 4—for open-door and other areas of communications—is in Appendix A.

CHAPTER 7

EMPLOYEE VALUE SYSTEMS

Human beings have a natural tendency to perceive all the world as they perceive themselves. And human resources professionals are not exempt from this phenomenon. Many human resources policies and practices have been created to meet the needs and satisfiers of their creators, and of executives and federal regulations. If it were true that all employees had the same orientations and value systems toward work as managers, then managers could indeed design successful programs for others.

Perhaps one of the best ways of describing the differences among people is to use the work of Dr. Clare Graves over his many years of research into levels of psychological existence. (1966-74) This research showed conclusively the dramatic differences in people's orientation toward the world, their view of life and their "values for working." It now appears that many of the problems of communication, productivity and unionization lie primarily in the significantly different value systems among managers, white collar, blue collar and other employee populations. Since people exist at different levels of psychological development, it is important to understand how these levels shape their values toward work and personnel policies and programs.

Value systems are how people perceive reality. These systems are the way individuals construct a model of the external reality that is seen and heard. Related to brain functioning and, possibly, to hemisphere dominance, such values are deeper and more profound than opinions or attitudes.

A value system isn't simply a behavior—it is *why* a person does what she or he does. Although the definition is too limiting, such a system could be a motivator. Value systems are implicit in the way a person uses words and symbols to understand and remember past and current events. Such systems develop through life's experiences and may change with time, depending on life's events.

Although value systems are deep seated, complex, and involved in perceptual and linguistic processes, they are relatively easy to understand for employee relations purposes. Such a statement may sound like a non sequitur, but managers can work with value systems on an applied, pragmatic basis without knowing everything that's going on in the brain of every employee.

In this brief introduction to six value systems of human existence (systems 2 through 7) found in our society, the single word label used for each value system inadequately describes the syndrome it represents, but is used for convenience of discussion. Because system 1 applies to infants, people with serious brain deterioration, and people with certain psychopathic conditions, for the purposes of this book, it is excluded.

Value system 2—tribalistic. Beyond the reactive stage, people develop into a state of tribalism in which the values held come from a chieftain who may be a boss, spouse or parent. The content of work is not important, but the leadership from the boss/chieftain is. People who exist at the tribalistic level of psychological development prefer strong leadership, a boss who tells them what to do and provides recognition when the work is done properly. Money and the other things necessary in life are for the purposes of existing. The formal education level of the tribalistic individual is quite likely to be low. Our studies show that many low income employees are primarily tribalistic and few, if any, professionals or others with advanced education and reasonable affluence are significantly tribalistic.

It is quite likely that administrators will develop programs that are fundamentally inappropriate to the tribalistic employee population. For example, tribalistic employees respond best to simple graphic and personalized communication. They tend to read little but do respond to pictures and appreciate eye-to-eye communication. As a result, many companies' employee handbooks are completely inappropriate to the tribalistic person's communication orientation.

Tribalistic employees prefer routine tasks and find a great deal of satisfaction in repetitive tasks that have a rhythmic routine. It is perhaps fortunate that 25 percent of the employee population is primarily tribalistic because industry offers so many tribalistic jobs. It would be a disservice to place a tribalistic person in a job with excessive task variety or job enlargement. The tribalistic employee should be placed with a good chieftain and other employees who hold the same values.

The area of performance appraisal systems is another likely to miss the orientation of the tribalistic value. Performance appraisal practices for these employees need to be designed so that the leader may correlate them with the values of the tribe. This means that the responsibility for designing performance appraisal systems and carrying out the procedures must be group centered and determined by the immediate supervisor. Here the relationship to the boss and the group is more appraised than the individual meritorious productivity of one person.

Pay and benefits for these employees should be based on automatic increases determined by the immediate supervisor and related to seniority and length of membership in the tribe or the super-tribe, the corporation. Merit pay approaches and individual piece rate systems are perceived as irrelevant. As far as benefits are concerned, any attempt to explain the details of the hospital/surgical plan is inappropriate because this employee's orientation toward benefits is receiving the "benefit of the benefit" at the time when it is needed.

Motivation centers on recognition from the boss for doing a good job, not from the job itself. Continuous "stroking" is needed, not job enrichment. As long as management ensures good quality supervision, these employees will respond with job satisfaction, loyalty to the boss and high productivity. They want to get along—not ahead. While the needs and wants of the tribalistic employee in regard to placement, communication, performance appraisal, pay and benefit administration and supervision may not feel good to management because of differing values, they feel good to system 2 people.

Value system 3—egocentric. This employee is the rugged individualist who is tough, aggressive and often a source of great unhappiness to managers and supervisors. Because they tend to be suspicious and to engage in disruptive behavior at work, the egocentric employees need jobs that do not tie them down and bosses who can control their behavior. Egocentric individuals place themselves ahead of others and generally have difficulty living within the constraints of society, business policy and ethics. Their mild paranoia makes them difficult to deal with and very sensitive to what they perceive as discrimination.

Communications to the egocentric must be direct, authoritarian and explain the consequences of good and bad behavior. As with the tribalistic, the printed word is not the most appropriate form of communication, but rather direct contact from the boss. With these employees there is a very high probability that communications will be rejected as a fake, artificial "rip off."

Many organizations may choose to screen egocentrics out entirely since they have been shown to have a propensity for disrupting the workforce, filing charges of discrimination and engaging in militant union activity. An egocentric employee requires a job with tight control, close supervision, continuous observation and a boss capable of exercising authority and power. Egocentrics do find satisfaction in individualistic jobs, one-of-a-kind jobs, dangerous jobs or jobs which require a great deal of physical toughness and ability. Managers must learn to deal with these employees effectively, for if all egocentrics were simply screened out, a very large problem would be created for society. To some degree, this has already occurred.

Performance appraisal for these employees must be individualistic, must come from the boss and should be given on a regular basis—not at six-month or annual performance review schedules. Because the egocentric view of the future resembles that of the tribalistic—from paycheck to paycheck—writing things down for discussion may not be appropriate. The feedback loop is too long to generate response. Treating egocentrics properly is difficult as they are always convinced that they are being underpaid and, if given the opportunity, could do more. This is conceivable but frustrating. Pinpoint rates or automatic increases on a seniority basis are probably the best forms of compensation as they leave less room for discussion, negotiation and perception of unfairness. Benefit programs are also of little interest to egocentrics as many programs require increased seniority to get increased benefits.

Our studies have shown that egocentrics have the highest turnover rate of all value systems—they always become dissatisfied with the boss, the work, the company and move on or simply drop out of the workforce until it is financially necessary to get another job. Motivation, therefore, is not related to job enrichment or recognition from the boss, but rather to the direction and power exercised by the supervisor to get productivity. Egocentrics prefer a boss who lets them be tough but is also tough. Supervisors of egocentrics must realize that they must be tougher than the employees.

Value system 4—conformist. Conformists have the classic work ethic—they are oriented toward duty, loyalty and what they "should" do. They have a high regard for the written word, policies, procedures, job descriptions and work duties. The good boss here is one who provides structure and direction. Consistent rules that everyone follows and little favoritism by supervisors are essential.

In employee communications, conformists respond to policy manuals, procedures, duty lists and "the book." Communications may take the interpersonal form, but the "shoulds" and "oughts" must be emphasized. System 4 people want to understand the logic and rationale of policies and procedures so they can assure themselves that everything is as it ought to be.

Selection and placement for conformists can be handled by the standard employee relations practices traditionally used by most organizations. Managers should not look for creativity from system 4 people and performance appraisal for them is in the best traditions of the field. Measurement of objective productive output versus job descriptions and externally imposed criteria are most meaningful to conformist employees. Performance appraisals must be conducted, documented and completed on a regular and timely basis. For conformists, performance appraisal and the opportunity for advancement are distinctly separate subjects, since employees trust management to do the job of selecting people for promotions.

Performance appraisal for this value system reinforces loyalty and the recognition of seniority and meeting performance objectives set by the supervisor. Pay and benefits should emphasize seniority and longevity with the organization. The conformist views pay as being earned through hard work and is disturbed when others who have not worked hard or made a contribution to the organization's performance receive increases. Although merit increases may be used, highly leveraged bonus systems are inappropriate unless they are granted almost as a right of position and rank and recognize status more than individual meritorious performance.

Fringe benefits are very important for they provide security from a benevolent organization and should increase gradually with length of service. Conformists believe that they have worked hard for what they have and that they deserve some good breaks; they respect an organization that takes care of its people through benefit programs. They have a high regard for the employee handbook, particularly the sections which give detailed explanations of various insurance, pension and vacation programs. It is important to have well-designed and consistently administered pay and benefit programs for systems 2, 3 and 4, as they respect structure and authority.

Motivation is primarily a response to job responsibility, loyalty and the structure of the organizational hierarchy. Intrinsic job satisfaction is present so long as the job is well organized, clearly specified and duties are provided in written form. Achievement and individuality added by pure job enrichment are not key motivating factors for conformists. They respond instead to jobs that permit their strong classic work ethic to be expressed.

Value system 5—manipulative. Manipulators are materialistic in their orientation toward life and work. They like "wheeling and dealing," opportunities for advancement, greater income, higher prestige and room to carefully maneuver their career plans to achieve their goals. Opportunity to get ahead is the strongest motivator.

Communications are most meaningful when they stress opportunities for advancement, objectives of the institution and challenges for people who are willing to work hard and make a contribution in order to achieve the rewards of our socio-economic system. Written policies and procedures are not important and are often perceived as barriers to the accomplishment of work and the fulfillment of personal needs and goals. The manipulator likes to be in the know and will often arrange to find out what is happening before official announcements and even influence the form and content of the communications from top management. Manipulators push the limits of communication. In their own communications to others they may engage in manipulation of the facts, which they justify through "flexible ethics."

Selection and placement must be concerned primarily with the opportunities for future advancement and potential income levels. Manipulators are most frequently found in positions of leadership, i.e., management and professional activities. The manipulative materialistic value system could almost be called the managerial value system, since in the recent past as well as currently, it represents the most outstanding attribute of people in leadership positions. Performance appraisal for manipulators must be goal-oriented and wrapped into the organization's planning system. A management by objectives approach is most effective here.

Appraisal is quite important to manipulative performers and they often initiate these activities themselves. Opportunities should be provided for them to assess their own performance, compare this to the boss's judgment of performance, discuss the differences and receive immediate concrete feedback. The clearest form of feedback in performance appraisal situations is opportunity for advancement, career plans, career goals and significant pay increases. Pay is extremely important to the manipulators because of their materialistic orientation. Seniority increases in pay are not as effective as merit; however, it is possible to integrate the manipulative value system with some of the others by placing the manipulative individual on a base rate structure which takes care of maintenance needs. This provides basic income but, if permitted to leverage this through merit increases, incentive awards, cash bonuses and stock options, will give the opportunity for substantial amounts of money and have immediate reinforcing impact.

Benefit programs are not as important to manipulators as value systems 2 and 4. They respond primarily to a benefit program they perceive as providing benefits which increase with pay or programs which permit them to select how they shall spend their benefit money. They are interested in the opportunity to buy benefits through the cost-effective approach of group plans using their own additional payroll deduction.

Motivation for the manipulator is a case of high achievement orientation, opportunity for advancement and the money itself as a motivator. Many strong manipulative people are found in marketing and sales jobs and motivation by achievement, status and money itself are legendary within American business and industry. The other strong motivator is a job which can be approached like a business game. In fact, the playing of the business game is the prime motivator, with money as the number one scorekeeping device.

Value system 6—sociocentric. As the label implies, the sociocentric centers on people as the most important thing in society and within the organization. Interpersonal relationships, human relations, friendly supervision and harmony with the work group are key values. Sociocentrics perceive power structures in institutions as hurting people or the environment. The human element must always be added in communications. The relationships among people within the institution, how people help each other and how the institution helps society must be included. Employee newspapers must have the human interest angle and handbooks must stress actual case studies or examples of how programs have, in fact, benefited the people.

Selection and placement of sociocentrics is critical, for they prefer a group in which teamwork is possible, eye contact and verbal communication constant. Personal contact with the supervisor and a boss who is more of a peer than a traditional boss is important. There are many factory and white collar jobs to which sociocentrics can respond, but they should not be placed in jobs with heavy individual competition as manipulative persons should. Attention should be paid to facilities and working conditions so that these do not block the interpersonal relationships.

Performance appraisal for these employees may be conducted on a peer evaluation basis or simply an evaluation of the entire work group without singling out individuals for different appraisal ratings. If individual ratings are necessary, supervisors should emphasize the human relations aspect of the individual's performance as well as the productivity, show how improving interpersonal relations can lead to higher productivity and how higher productivity benefits not only the work group but the institution and the public it serves. Even with individual performance appraisals the supervisor should be encouraged to meet with the entire group and discuss its overall performance as a group.

Pay and benefits are important, as they are to all value systems. Emphasizing pay differences and merit increases will be perceived as creating a "dog-eat-dog" world by the institution and the boss. Sociocentrics would pay everyone the same amount and give everyone exactly the same benefit program, regardless of position or length of service. Their orientation toward pay and benefits is usually the socialistic view. They will accept longevity and seniority-oriented pay increases just as systems 2, 3 and 4, but merit pay is not appropriate for the bulk of this system. The only form of merit pay would be merit for the group in group incentive plans where everyone shares equally.

Motivation for the sociocentric comes from social relations, interpersonal transactions and the egalitarian democratic value. Individual achievement and responsibility are not key motivators. Job enrichment conducted with sociocentrics should emphasize recognition by the boss for a good job by the group and personal growth as a part of humanity. The most powerful motivator for a sociocentric, however, is the opportunity to get paid for helping people.

Value system 7—existential. People with this relatively new value system, the existential, are mostly concerned with themselves as individuals but without the hostility and negative effect found in system 3 and sometimes in system 5. These are the people for whom job enrichment and meaningful tasks are absolutely essential. Many of the theories of leadership, motivation and organizational structure are perfect fits here. (These theories, as we have found in our research, are only partially compatible with some value systems and essentially inappropriate for others.) The opportunity to solve problems and engage in meaningful task variety which demands challenge, imagination, initiative and creativity are the working values of the existential.

Communications geared to existentials must relate to their favorite word—"why?" They have a high regard for the language and are not afraid of words and engage in many semantic games, exercises and diversions. Existentials will read printed material, although they do not take the printed word as law as will conformists. They are most interested in communications which pull together all aspects of the situation to show the long range effects of a course of action. They may tend to disregard policy manuals if they think them inappropriate or irrelevant to the immediate situation.

Selecting existentials is a very difficult task. They will refuse jobs that do not have challenge, opportunity and intellectual stimulation. Placement is also very critical. Even though the task content may be appropriate, they operate well only under general supervision where they participate in goal setting and in the formulation of strategies for achieving those goals. Furthermore, the style of supervision must also be existential or possibly mildly manipulative since essentially the existential requires no supervision. They are quite likely to either turn off or turn over if placed under a highly authoritarian conformist. They respond best to internal systems (such as job posting and bidding) which permit them to seek the type of work they want as opposed to being placed by someone in authority. Given access to information about jobs they will tend to seek out jobs which fit them best and resist regimentation.

Existentials tend to conduct their own self-generated performance appraisals constantly. The performance of the boss and the organization often appear to be appraised rather than the behavior and productivity of existentials themselves. Self-initiated performance appraisal with discussion with the boss is most important. However, numerical and work rating scales that attempt to categorize the job performance of the existential will be resisted. They may prefer to have a conversation without documentation. Classic performance appraisal will be disregarded by the existential and should be avoided if at all possible.

Pay and benefits are important to the existential. However, money itself is not as important as what existentials do with it. They recognize that money is necessary to operate in our society, but having the money is not as important as what money can buy—the freedom and opportunity to be oneself. Existentials will accept the seniority or longevity-based pay system and some general form of bonus or incentive award, but they resist being manipulated by compensation schemes they perceive as attempts to induce them to do things they believe are inappropriate or inefficient. Benefits are accepted but at no time do they ever form "golden handcuffs" that keep the existential loyal or prevent him from quitting to pursue a more meaningful task elsewhere.

Compensation in all forms is necessary but not sufficient to get productivity from the existential. The key is job enrichment. For here a major motivator is the sense of achievement that comes from solving difficult problems and reaching personal goals that are also important to the institution. The opportunity to grow, learn, change, make a contribution, explore new territory and at all times to be original and creative are the most powerful factors. This new breed of individuals make a striking contrast with other value systems which have existed for a longer period of time. However, the key to personnel administration with existentials, as with all value systems, is flexibility.

Summary

As we have described, if it's right for management, it may be wrong for the rest of the employees. Companies need to follow a new concept and not design programs that feel good to management because there is a high probability that they will feel bad to many others. What Human Resources and other management groups may have been doing is designing programs for themselves and their bosses. (Research indicates that the attributes of managers in terms of values are essentially those of executives.) Whether or not employee relations programs are designed for the wide range of values or whether we find ways to involve supervision and the rank and file employee in the design of programs is a matter of choice.

It is not necessary to have completely different programs for each value system. For example, it is not necessary to have six different benefit programs. Not only is it not feasible, it is not important. However, these benefit programs must be communicated in six different ways so that each value system can tune in to its own wave length. It is not necessary to have six different forms of pay. Seniority-related or longevity-oriented pay will work with all systems with the exception of system 5 (which does need the addition of the individual bonus or award) and to some degree bonuses and awards for existentials, but they have much less impact. In other words, there is a difference between being "paid enough" and being "paid more."

Appraising performance requires flexibility and it is possible six different systems may be required. However, this is possible and practical for it is nothing more than providing six different forms or devising a procedure which can be used according to the values of the individuals being appraised. High conformity of performance appraisal systems will miss the majority of employees, so flexibility is essential. Selection and placement flexibility is critical. Because human resources administrators are often most attracted to people who have the same values, they might place them in a job which is better suited to a different value system.

Communications is the key. With all of the flexibility that we might conceivably build into selection, placement, performance review, pay, benefits and job content, communications must have a full range of values. We must find

Employee Value Systems

multiple words, multiple channels, multiple processes for communication so that each value can respond and comprehend in its own natural style.
This is both our challenge and our opportunity.

Dos and Don'ts by Value Systems

	Communication	Job Design	Management Systems and Procedures	Growth Opportunity	Pay and Benefits
2 Tribalistic	DO pass information through the boss DON'T depend on the printed word	DO provide a benevolent, protective, autocratic boss DON'T impose "planning and controlling" onto "doing"	DO recognize that the "Boss" IS the system DON'T expect compliance with any other system but the boss	DO make sure the boss gives guidance for advancement DON'T require long range career planning	DO make compensation automatic DON'T use merit pay or complex benefit programs
3 Egocentric	DO tell employees what's in it for them personally DON'T use logic or folksy appeals	DO make them feel super-important and powerful DON'T fail to keep them busy and under control	DO explain the consequences of noncompliance DON'T leave any loop-holes	DO make promotion contingent on good performance DON'T let them con you on their abilities	DO use piece rates or automatic increases DON'T defer payment
4 Conformist	DO use the printed word and stress "shoulds and oughts" DON'T be inconsistant or leave out details	DO write detailed job descriptions and duties DON'T let him lose sight of the purpose and goal	DO use formalized "Standard Operating Procedures" DON'T expect any originality or creativity	DO provide step-by-step career plans DON'T promote until employee feels he or she has earned it	DO improve pay and benefits for seniority and loyalty DON'T use merit pay or competitive bonuses
5 Manipulative	DO imply personal career advantages DON'T quote what "the book says"	DO turn work into a "management by objectives game" DON'T fail to specify the limits and boundaries	DO leave room for some "wheeling and dealing" DON'T forget to audit occasionally	DO let them run the corporate maze DON'T plan career goals and paths for them	DO tie awards to achieving objectives DON'T expect benefits to get loyalty
6 Sociocentric	DO make people the most important subject DON'T oversell profits and production	DO set work up for group interaction DON'T let "participation" overshadow productivity	DO humanize the system DON'T let group consensus block implementation	DO provide opportunities for exposure to more people DON'T cause competition with friends	DO keep pay rates in line with the group DON'T try to get performance through money
7 Existential	DO simply make information available DON'T quote what "Management says"	DO get involvement in problem solving and goal setting DON'T fail to get clear commitment	DO provide broad guidelines only DON'T expect obedience to inflexible systems	DO provide movement in any direction DON'T be surprised if they refuse promotion	DO put intrinsic job interest ahead of money DON'T try to make benefits into "golden handcuffs"

Why Employees Stay Is More Critical Than Why They Leave*

Many personnel executives spend a great amount of time and money investigating the causes of employee turnover, particularly through exit interviews. If a company can identify the reasons for terminations and departures, the theory goes, it can remove some of the causes for employee dissatisfaction. There are, however, two shortcomings with this traditional practice:

- It looks at only why people quit. Why not also look at the reasons others stay? The reasons why people stay are just as important as the reasons for leaving. One individual may stay in a job for the same reason another leaves.
- Exit interviews also assume there is a correlation between job dissatisfaction and turnover. A low turnover rate presumes that employees are happy and consequently productive; this is not necessarily the case. The mere fact an employee stays is not as important as *why* that person remains.

Studies of the attitudes of tens of thousands of employees in more than five hundred organizations investigated the reasons employees stay and proper ways to encourage retention. From anonymous questionnaires and selected interviews this is the picture that emerges:

Why do employees stay? Employees tend to stay where they are until some force causes them to leave, in other words "inertia." As in physics, a body will remain as it is until acted upon by an external force. Two factors inside organizations and two outside make people stay. Job satisfaction and satisfaction with the working environment produces the internal inertia and is directly affected by the positive or negative correlation between the employee's personal value system and that of management. A disparity between personal and organizational values reduces the desire to stay, while compatibility between these two values increases the desire to stay.

The external factors that increase inertia include perceptions of other job opportunities and personal and family reasons. Some employees stay because they like the schools or the neighborhood, but what if both of these deteriorate and become less appealing? Other job opportunities become more attractive.

Other employees report they stay in an unpleasant job because they could not leave the community in which they or their spouse was born and spent all of their lives. Despite low job satisfaction, they stay.

Want to stay versus have to stay. Progressive management should try to improve retention by reinforcing positive reasons for staying, while at the same time making it easier for people who are staying for negative reasons—

---

* By Charles L. Hughes and Vincent Flowers (1987). Reprinted with the permission of *Personnel Journal*, Costa Mesa, CA; all rights reserved.

negative to both employer and employee—to quit. Turnover *quality*, as opposed to turnover *quantity*, might improve.

Improving employee retention will be more effective over the long run than the ordinary, negative approach of simply reducing turnover. The key is improving attitudes about the work itself, supervisor competence, confidence in the fairness of management, workgroup cooperation, consistency in treatment, feedback about performance, opportunities to get ahead, and other positive aspects that relate to the work context. Work content factors—those aspects of the job inside the organization—include pay, benefits, facilities, attendance rules, and other environmental factors.

External factors include outside job opportunities, the community, financial obligations, family ties, and even the annual weather patterns. As a result of the combinations of external and internal factors influencing employees' job decisions, employees can be identified as one of four types:

(1) *Turnovers* are not happy with their jobs, have few external reasons to stay and will leave at the first opportunity. Employees may not start out in this position, but a gradual erosion of their inertia causes them to slide into this area.

(2) *Turn-offs* are candidates for union, employee relations, and productivity problems. These employees have negative attitudes about their jobs and stay because of golden handcuffs. They may

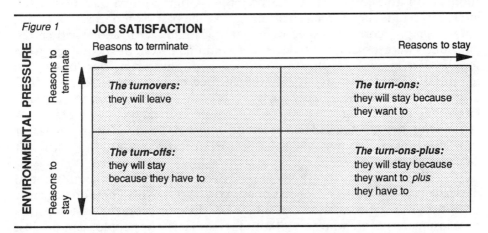

feel they are too old to start over again and are locked in by benefit programs and high rates of pay. Productivity may suffer.

(3) *Turn-ons* have positive attitudes and remain with the company for reasons almost exclusively associated with the work itself. From management's point of view, as well as the individual employee's, this is the most desirable situation.

If management actions lower attitudes and the positive, work-related reasons to stay, turnover will probably jump. Because the turn-ons are not affected by environmental factors, they will not stay without continual job satisfaction.

(4) *Turn-on-plus* employees are likely to stay for the long run because they have work and environmental satisfaction. A short-term drop in satisfaction does not lead to resignation. If attitudes drop permanently, however, these employees become turn-offs. This does not raise turnover, but increases employee relations problems.

The traditional approach to measuring and understanding terminations has focused on turnovers. These employees generally represent a small percentage of the total employee population, therefore, placing retention efforts on them exclusively ignores the reasons the majority of the workforce stays with the company. Employers wanting to improve their working environments should stop assuming that exit interviews provide a meaningful picture of why other employees stay.

An anonymous attitude survey was used to identify where employees fit in the matrix (Figure 1) of "having to stay versus wanting to stay." This survey covered twenty factor-analyzed statements to which individuals could respond "agree, disagree, ?, not sure." It explored job satisfaction, supervision, management, advancement, working conditions, pay, benefits, communication, performance expectations, job security, favoritism, use of skills, workgroup cooperation, rules, freedom to do the job well, plus an item on whether the individual had looked for another job during the past six months.

Simply, correlations between each attitude factor and whether the individuals were looking or not looking to terminate from their company were sought. For example, if they are satisfied with any factor, but looking to terminate anyway, they are classified as "turned-on" by that factor, but "not locked in." Conversely, if individuals are "dissatisfied" by any of the attitude factors and not looking for another job, they are "turned off" by that factor or factors *plus* they are "locked in." If an individual is "satisfied" with any factor and "not looking" to quit, then that factor, or factors, "turn on" but don't "lock in" that employee.

Employees stay for three reasons, two positive (want to, and want to plus have to) and one negative (do not want to, but have to). These do not show up as turnover statistics or on exit interviews. In short, sometimes companies have lost many people who are still with them, so it is why people *stay,* not just why they leave that must be considered.

Employee Value Systems Sway Employees' Job Decisions

In looking at attitudes, researchers find that what stimulates some individuals drives others crazy and vice versa. It's a matter of each individual's value system. Not everyone finds the same satisfaction from the same work.

Some prefer a variety of tasks and others prefer routines. Some want a participative management style and some truly want to be told what to do and make no decisions. Some seek promotion and some prefer to stay where they are.

These individual differences in value systems are not unusual. Research has easily identified situations in which two individuals occupy similar jobs with the same supervisor, the same pay and benefits, working conditions, and so on. But one employee was satisfied and one *was* dissatisfied—*by the same things*.

Research indicates that tribalistic and egocentric employees usually stay at their jobs because they are locked in by external factors. That is, they cannot leave because they have no place to go, regardless of whether they like their current situation. They show a high degree of inertia and so remain where they are—whether they're satisfied or dissatisfied.

Low turnover, in this case, does not reflect job satisfaction. It is necessary to look at attitudes to find out. The internal organization reasons to stay are primarily pay and benefits more than intrinsic work satisfaction and management style. Low turnover proves nothing but low turnover; *why* they stay is the key.

Conformist and sociocentric employees are about equal on internal and external reasons to stay. They stay because they cannot leave and they also stay because they want to. The internal reasons to remain with their companies are pay and benefits *plus* intrinsic work satisfaction and appreciation of the management style of the organization. In short, they stay for traditional reasons, and they stay with a company during short-term difficulties and dissatisfaction. In these instances, then, a company can have low turnover, but high dissatisfaction. To presume morale is high because turnover is low is a serious error. These employees will seek union representation rather than quit.

Manipulative and existential employees stay almost exclusively for positive reasons. They are far less vulnerable to being locked in. Their turn-ons come mainly from positive motivation relating to their working situation and seldom from external factors. Manipulative employees stay primarily for factors relating to advancement and pay, whereas existential employees stay mainly for intrinsic work satisfaction and to use their skills and abilities. They pay little attention to external factors and keep their resumes up to date so they can leave quickly if they become dissatisfied.

The Quality of Employees Retained Supersedes the Quantity Lost

From the analysis of value systems it becomes apparent that quantity of turnover is not as important as is the quality. Is the company keeping the people it needs for the future? To find out why employees stay employers must ask those who stay why they choose to do so.

Many people stay merely because their value system tends to lock them in. It's in everyone's interest (except labor unions) to search out and eliminate the negative aspects of their jobs that turn off those workers and to accentuate the positive aspects of the work. For those employees whose value systems demand a positive environment and who are not locked in by negatives or the external factors, the positive must also be accentuated and the negatives eliminated. The following six-step process identifies ways to accomplish this.

Step 1) Accept that value systems of employees may be quite different from those of management. What satisfies one group may likely turn off another and vice versa. Realize and accept that it is not a matter of right and wrong, but simply of differences.

Step 2) Be willing to look at employee relations policies and procedures from the perspective of the receiving end of the process, not the design end. The right policy for pay, attendance, promotion, and the rest is what works best for the people in the organization, not what is preferred by the personnel department or upper management.

Step 3) Ask people why they stay, either through a survey or in interviews, and listen carefully. Ask them their opinion or attitude about a particular policy or management practice and be willing to redesign it so it matches a prevalent value system.

Step 4) Communicate whatever policies the company has in a language style that is compatible with the employees' value systems. Learn to listen in a style befitting the employees' value systems, and respond accordingly. Ask the supervisors how to do this. They are closer to the employees and probably already know how their people think.

Step 5) When hiring and placing employees, consider the value systems of the stimulated people who stay and match the new people to their value systems. Try to fit new employees naturally to the company's internal environmental value system. Avoid hiring people whose value systems resemble those employees who are locked in and turned off.

Step 6) Always remember that eliminating the negatives and accentuating the positives is a process, not a program. Employee involvement in the process is key; always fully involve supervisors before anything is changed. People are more likely to believe in what they help create.

Toward Existential Management

If we move away from traditional management, with its tendency to "mirror" values, toward existentialism in management, we may find some answers to the dilemma of meeting values of people and the goals of the organization at the same time. When there is a mismatch between the value systems and the job content, it is most likely that alienation and low productivity will result. One obvious answer may be the proper placement of people in jobs where their values and job content match. It is conceivable that you could test employees to determine their value systems, then identify the job content value and place people accordingly. This may be a partial solution to the problem. A second prescription may be to educate managers to understand and appreciate the varying value systems among their workforce and attempt to accommodate others' values in their design of management systems and procedures. This is certainly a step in the right direction and a prerequisite for the ultimate long-range solution.

The ultimate long-range solution is to provide an existential management approach in which managers determine the goals of the organization, but the people influence the systems and procedures by which the goals are achieved. The existential role of managers is (1) to set goals for the organization, (2) to share with employees information about methods, constraints, and resources limits, and (3) to provide the opportunity for employees to become involved and participate in the design of the systems and procedures they will use to accomplish the goals for the management.

Employee Involvement—Means, Not an End

Employee involvement has been a prescription for many years, but the reason managers used participative management was to try to "love" people into productivity. That is, it has been a sociocentric idea applied to manipulative organizations. We are not proposing that involvement occur simply because managers should love employees; that is not a relevant factor. We are proposing, however, a systematic approach in which individuals or groups who have disparate value systems participate in the design of the systems and procedures, including work content, assembly line operations, and employee relations programs. When these employee-designed systems and procedures are used to manage the employees themselves, the systems and procedures will be compatible with the employees' values, and this leads to productive employee behavior and achieves the goals originally established by management.

In summary, we encourage employee involvement techniques, not as an end in themselves, but as a means of designing systems and procedures that permit both productivity and job satisfaction.

The use of ad hoc committees has been tried a number of places, usually with outstanding results. We have already mentioned the case of an employee performance appraisal system designed by corporate Human Resources staff that was met with attitudes ranging from indifference to alienation. When several ad hoc committees were formed to design their own system to meet their own needs and values, the new system was met with a high degree of satisfaction by the supervisors and the people they supervised. The reason? The system was more adequately designed to suit their value systems than any system that staff experts were able to design.

In another case, productivity was increased through participation of workers in the design of manufacturing systems. A group of assemblers on a complicated piece of electronic hardware were following the system specified by management and industrial engineers. In the beginning, more than 100 hours were required to assemble a unit. Under pressure to increase productivity, the supervisors applied every management technique with which they were familiar (increased pressure, emotional appeals, greater attention to people on the job, improved human relations), none of which caused the efficiency of the organization to improve. As a last resort, the supervisors turned to the formation of ad hoc teams, who were asked to help solve production problems and set goals for higher productivity. (The format of these meetings followed the model originally developed by Allan Mogensen; known as "work simplification (it predated "quality circles" by decades.)") This is essentially a technique for do-it-yourself industrial engineering in which supervisors are trained in motion and time economy, conference leadership, and flow-charting. They then share these techniques with the workers, who apply them to the improvement in efficiency and productive output. Many people today feel that "work simplification" is inappropriate because the very name implies that it moves in the opposite direction of the job-enrichment concept. Without going into all the aspects of the team problem-solving approach, suffice it to say that the work group and their supervisors got three times the output that industrial engineering expected. Additionally, attitudes improved, and turnover and absenteeism declined during the one-and-a-half-year life of this problem-solving and goal-setting project.

We could cite many other examples where involvement and participation of employees in determining the means by which goals will be achieved not only has positive impact on attitudes, but also yields systems and jobs that match the values of people—plus better productivity. With the competitive pressure for world-class productivity and quality, intelligent employee involvement is essential to get the needed "continuous improvement."

Summary and Key Points

Many factors in the maintenance of unionfree status are affected by people's perceptions. The essential ingredient of good employee communications for the maintenance of unionfree status is the understanding that rank-and-file employees have values, words, language, perceptions, and attitudes that are different from each other and quite distinct from those of management. Although some professional employees have values that overlap those of managers, they too, are in a different situation in regard to communications, job design, policies and procedures, pay and benefits, and working conditions and facilities. In essence, this means that we need an approach tailored to the values, needs, perceptions, and motivation patterns of various employee populations.

In attitude surveys of over 550 organizations comprising a total of more than a half-million employees, we find the more *manipulative* the management, the more miserable the employees. The *good news* is that slightly more than half of the employees do have confidence and trust in their leaders, because the more *existential* the management, the more positive the attitudes. *Reality-oriented* managers are more psychologically mature, self-aware and confident, and encourage dignity and respect toward employees. They do not play games to win, so the employees are never losers. Existential play is infinite, no winning or losing. It has no destination, only direction, and the direction is toward an always moving horizon. There are no boundaries, only limited vision. There is no power, only strength. Existentially, there is no need to win. In an infinite game, no one competes.

CHAPTER 8

JOB DESIGN

There is a great deal of concern in management currently about the concept of "job enrichment." Although job enrichment is a worthwhile social movement from any viewpoint, including both job satisfaction and improvement in productivity, these programs too often reflect the values of management, with insufficient consideration for the value systems of the employees whose jobs are being enriched. The concepts of motivation apply, but the power of the various motivation factors such as growth, achievement, responsibility, recognition, and job content varies according to the value system of the individual. Many people are quite satisfied with relatively routine jobs; others must have a meaningful task in order to be motivated, satisfied, and productive.

If a person is going to spend many years at a job, it should be suited to her or his needs. It is difficult for managers to know how to design jobs for employees other than managers. Therefore, the use of involvement techniques that permit employees to rearrange the work flow, improve productivity, reduce costs, and find tasks that are more meaningful has value here, just as it does in the area of employee communications. For example, workers with a tribalistic value system, have a preference for routine, repetitive tasks. Given the opportunity to participate in job design, these people will define highly structured tasks and will attempt to get their job satisfaction through things other than variety of job content. On the other hand, egocentrics do not like any type of work, or even working itself, but do so out of basic economic necessity and, therefore, will perform any job as long as there is close supervision. The people with manipulative values are found primarily in the management and professional populations. The content of their work is critical, and job enrichment is vital to their motivation, as well as to minimize the risk of managerial or professional unions. As we move higher on the values development scale, the need for variety in work increases. When it is provided, variety tends to result in higher productivity.

Employee involvement in the design of jobs, and procedures for accomplishing it, are essential, because by this means the value system of the particular group will be given effect rather than having the needs and motivation patterns of management personnel imposed upon groups of employees who may have totally different perceptions of the world of work.

Perhaps the most essential ingredients are the traditional concepts of fair treatment and consistency of administration of policies and procedures by supervisors. Since supervision and management control the content of work for employees to such an extent, the quality of the supervision is essential in both productivity motivation and the maintenance of unionfree status. For this and many other reasons, adequate and effective supervisor training is a necessity. Consideration should be given to the concept that many supervisors could perform better if their own jobs were designed in a manner that would enable them to deal more effectively with employees. In analyzing the problem of supervisor training, it is first necessary to analyze the supervisor's job to see if effective, competent supervision of other people is possible. Here again is an opportunity for participation by supervisors in the design of their own job content.

Although managers determine the objectives of the organization, employee participation in determining job design becomes a strategic means of achieving managerial goals. This holds significant promise for the future as a way of both counteracting unionization and improving productivity growth rates. A number of experiments, as well as the continuing practices of many corporations, have shown that it is possible, through participative methods in the design of jobs and the methodology for achieving organizational goals, to attain significant increases in productivity in the range of 10 to 30 percent or more. When employees participate in the design of their work methodology, they become, in effect, adjuncts to management—and people do not organize against themselves.

Improvement Through Involvement

When the workforce is involved in the effort to improve the effectiveness of the organization, not only does the resulting economic efficiency permit the payment of improved wages and benefits, but the job satisfaction that results tends to decrease employee concern for such environmental factors as working conditions and job security. There are a number of methods for accomplishing improvement through involvement; most of them are concerned with group problem-solving and goal-setting techniques. Not only do group problem-solving and method-improvement techniques often result in productivity improvements and increase job satisfaction for employees, they can also make a significant improvement in the content of the supervisor's role. Certainly, anything that can be done to improve the place and status of first-line supervisors in the corporation as well as their own job satisfaction is essential to productivity and the maintenance of unionfree status. Although the design of jobs is not a complete answer to "union-proofing" an organization, it represents a kind of communication through the language of action that can have a significant impact. When employees as well as managers and supervisors are motivated to achieve the goals of the organization, there is little reason for them to become involved in such anti-corporation movements as unionization.

Essential to the concept of improvement through involvement and job design is the definition of what constitutes "the job." If the job is narrowly defined as the routine performed at the work station, the definition may be too limited to permit sufficient employee involvement with the activities of the corporation. Although not everyone needs a job that is full of excitement and variety, showing consideration of employees as human beings by consulting them and permitting and encouraging them to participate in the operation of the company in the area in which they work has an overriding symbolic consequence. Employees who are unable or unwilling to make significant contributions to the improvement of their performance or the organization's effectiveness are not necessarily antiorganization; they may lack sufficient knowledge or training to be able to accomplish the task of involvement. Nevertheless, there is much to be said simply for having been given the opportunity to participate. The company's recognition that the individual exists may be sufficient. Furthermore, management support of group problem-solving and goal-setting activities gives a challenge and opportunity to supervisors to reconsider their role as leaders of people as well as to participate in activities that bring people closer together and improve communications.

Performance Expectations

Qualitative Goals with supporting quantitative standards are key to both organizational and individual excellence. Qualitative goals determine the direction in which the organization will move; quantitative standards are the roads on which the organization can move. It makes no sense to build roads when you don't know where they should go.

A shared belief system or philosophy is essential to achieving and maintaining excellence. These beliefs or goals must be shared among all employees and upheld and reinforced through actions as well as words. Top management plays a particularly critical role in reinforcing qualitative goals—if they don't practice what they preach, neither will anyone else.

Qualitative goals must not only be reinforced daily by the actions of top management, the supervisor, the workgroup and interdependent departments, they must also be an integral part of the performance appraisal system. Unfortunately, the state of the art in employee performance appraisal does more to destroy excellence than to promote it. It is very difficult to generate and uphold shared beliefs when the performance rating system does not reinforce them with tangible means of measurement, or the measurement system reinforces behaviors incongruent with the organization's philosophies.

Most organizations measure employees by a single set of performance factors that usually do not recognize job content differences and tend to rate personality instead of performance. In addition, few organizations have performance appraisal systems that recognize the supervisor's effect on employee performance. The immediate supervisor is a powerful role model, and his or her guidance, support and actions may have as much an effect on employee performance as the individual employee's skills.

Managers at all levels generally agree that performance standards are key to productivity, pay systems and promotional opportunities and help prevent legal disputes. Yet, although managers agree in principle that specific, distinct, measurable standards are necessary, when given the opportunity to overhaul existing performance appraisal systems, they merely adopt a variation of the same old theme.

Problems with performance standards are further aggravated by the use of five-point ratings scales that tolerate torpidity. A five-point scale gives three opportunities to accept less than top-notch performance. A ten-point scale gives eight. Lay the forced distribution curve on top of five or ten-point scales and instead of pursuing excellence, you perpetuate mediocrity. A binary rating—Required Performance and Unacceptable Performance—is all that is needed to promote excellence.

If there is a way to once and for all solve performance appraisal problems, it lies in delegating the responsibility of custom designing performance standards for each different job to supervisors and their employees. Managers must limit their involvement in the design of the performance standards system to stating the goals, roles, rules and rewards and letting the users—supervisors and their employees—figure out the rest. Industrial engineers, union bargainers and corporate staffers with their entourage of management consultants must be banned from the process.

A caveat: Individual employees cannot set standards for their jobs until managers and supervisors have set quantitative standards supporting company qualitative goals for their own jobs. Role models are mandatory. What you set is what you get. By setting standards with their workgroup, supervisors convey faith in each person's integrity. It's a law of nature that when you know someone believes in you, you do not want to let that person down. Again, it's a self-fulfilling prophecy. Tell people they are good and expect them to show it, and they will! (For Self-Audit 5, on performance standards, see Appendix A.)

A Process for Defining Excellence

This process, sometimes called the existential process, for determining the means and measurements of performance excellence has certain inherent assumptions. If the manager does not agree with these assumptions, the process will not work. Employees will view it as just another gimmick or manipulative program.

Managers and Supervisors must assume that:

- people are good and want to be productive.
- employee involvement is the key to achieving excellence.
- "management" is a process that, when guided by integrity, builds trust and instills the desire to excel.
- an organizational goal is to maximize individual human potential.
- the value systems of employees match the values inherent in their jobs.

Job Design

- the purpose of setting job standards is not to be punitive but to define excellence.

If management sincerely believes these assumptions, and employees have confidence in their ability to be fair, you are ready to begin this process for defining excellence in performance.

1. Top management establishes an organizational philosophy and makes all goals explicit throughout the organization.
2. Share these goals with all employees. Explain the how and why behind them and why commitment is needed from every employee. Then describe the process you are about to undertake. Ask employees to do the following:
    (a) make a list of their individual duties and responsibilities as they see them;
    (b) rank order them according to importance, and list why each is important;
    (c) make a list of the duties and responsibilities they need their supervisors to fulfill to support them in their jobs and maintain a positive work environment.
3. Supervisors or managers do the same for each job.
4. Supervisors meet with individual employees or groups of employees. Go through every duty and responsibility on both lists to see whether they are consistent with the stated organizational philosophy. If there are any inconsistencies, mutually work out solutions by changing either the behavior or the goal. Until duties and responsibilities are consistent with organizational goals, it makes no sense to measure them.
5. Next, compare the two lists of duties and responsibilities and mutually determine a master list. Then, together determine a rank order of importance by discussing and documenting the "why" behind each duty and responsibility.
6. Work and rework the list and ranking until there is agreement on the duties and responsibilities and the meaning of the words used to describe them. Then, for each item on the merged list, mutually set performance measurements for both the employee and the supervisor. Some responsibilities may need only one criterion; others may require several. Keep at it until there is agreement on each factor. Carefully document the "why" and "how" behind each measurement and the reasoning behind using it as a measurement (this way, as things change over time, everyone will understand why certain measurements were originally set, and you can change them as situations change). After setting each measurement, ask yourselves "Is this behavior and its measurement consistent with the goals of the organization?" If not, change the behavior, the measurement or both until any incongruencies are resolved.
7. Supervisors should meet with the employee when either one feels

the need to review and, if necessary, update the definition of excellence and its measurements.

Are Supervisors Authentic?

Few managers question the belief that the anointed workgroup leader, the first-line supervisor, is the key to positive attitudes, work quantity and quality, and communications with their workgroups, yet many managers fail to accept supervisors as "management." There is a lingering tendency in many organizations to invalidate the supervisor's authority and responsibility by failing to *openly* verify the supervisor's role. Supervisors are universally told by other members of management that their role is to select, train, communicate, motivate, achieve performance standards, correct employee relations problems, provide technical information, be a positive role model, perform other duties as assigned, etc., and supervisees are told to expect such from their "boss." With this kind of responsibility, the supervisory role *must be* confirmed as "management" by higher levels of management through delegation of authority and level of pay.

The first step toward authenticating the authority of the supervisor is for management to demonstrate its trust by permitting and encouraging supervisors to actually fulfill all the responsibilities assigned to them, and standing behind their decisions. Supervisors must always have the final decision when selecting new people for their team; they must define and help design the training they feel their people need; essentially all communication—upward, downward, oral and written—between management and nonmanagement employees must flow through them; they must play a leading role in designing a performance standards system for their teams, and their doors must be the first ones opened when solving employee relations problems.

It's fairly obvious that supervisors who fulfill such responsibilities are the nucleus of the organization. Virtually all employee activities revolve around the supervisor. Because of their central role, supervisors should always give other members of management the benefit of their counsel before anything affecting employee relations is decided. The role of first-line supervisor is among the most demanding in the organization, and leaders who can effectively handle the role are to be respected, encouraged and openly recognized as "management."

The second step toward authenticating the role of supervisor is to financially reward them for their crucial role in their workgroups' success. Many organizations tend to overlook the importance of the pay factor. We repeatedly hear managers of both unionfree and unionized facilities complain that competent people refuse promotions to supervision because they feel it does not pay—psychologically and financially—to assume "all the headaches."

In many cases, supervisors make the same money (or less!) as those they supervise, which tends to undermine their authority with their workgroup. In some organizations, a person actually has to take a pay cut to become a supervisor! During a union organizing drive, when the first-line supervisor's role moves from key to critical, it is very difficult for these supervisors to try to convince their people that the organization pays fairly.

As a general rule, supervisors should be paid *at least* 15 percent more than the people they supervise. We know of some organizations that pay as much as 20 percent more, and they have no trouble promoting good people into supervisory jobs. To determine where your organization stands, identify the top-rated pay class in each workgroup and determine the difference between it and the supervisor's pay. If the differential is not at least 15 percent, the supervisor's pay should be raised until it is. The differential must hold throughout the year, so if there is long-term scheduled overtime, supervisors must receive an overtime premium to maintain the differential.

Training Supervisors To Do *What?*

Supervisor training is often referred to as the "aspirin" of industry. When employee attitudes are poor or a quantity/quality problem develops, management gives supervisors two training programs and has them report back in the morning. This may provide temporary, symptomatic relief but will not resolve the residual problem any more than two aspirin will resolve a recurring headache. Any good doctor will tell you that treating the symptoms will not eradicate the cause.

"Train 'em!" is the typical management response when supervisors experience problems with morale, productivity, quality, attendance and turnover. But management generally fails to specify "what" supervisors should be trained to do. Are they to be trained to follow policies and practices that may somehow be directly contributing to the problem? Why is management so quick to assume there is a training problem? Before recommending training, management should follow the Bob Mager approach and ask, "Could they do it if they had a gun to their heads?" If the answer is "yes", training is not the problem.

Our experience has shown that most supervisors do an amazingly good job in spite of some of the inappropriate policies they are expected to work with. Many times the root of the problem is the severe flaws in the basic design of employee relations systems, and supervisors are left to grapple with policy/practice mismatches. It's also possible that supervisors don't follow official management-mandated policies because they don't understand why the policies were created and how they are supposed to work.

Performance standards are a classic example of a policy/practice mismatch. At this time the majority of performance appraisal systems and the attendant forms are created by management, promulgated by "Disneyland North" and furnished to supervisors with no involvement on the part of the supervisors and supervisees. They are not owned by the users, and when resistance to the system is encountered, management prescribes a training program for supervisors.

Another classic example is when supervisors have little or no input in hiring decisions. When productivity problems result, an outside consultant is called in as a broad spectrum antibiotic to deliver a "motivation and leadership seminar."

When was the last time anyone asked supervisors if they wanted or needed training? When was the last time supervisees requested that their supervisor be trained? When was the last time managers asked to be trained first? When have we investigated to see whether the policies management wants supervisors to use are appropriate? It's ironic. Managers frequently complain about "headquarters" devising and installing new management systems without first consulting them, but they feel it's acceptable for them to do the same thing to their supervisors.

Before attempting another supervisor training program, determine whether training is the problem. If it is, then define what supervisory behavior toward employees is desired. The key is to specify the desired behavior and ensure that job expectations clearly describe and reinforce this behavior. Next, examine the policies and tools provided to assess whether they promote or inhibit desired behavior. If there are anomalies in the system, change the system. If the system is changed and the desired behavior results, no training is necessary. If there is no behavioral change, even at "gunpoint," training is required, and the answer to "train them to do *what?*" is clear.

Coaching Versus Training

Traditional supervisor training programs too often lack a clear purpose. "What" the manager expects the supervisor to be able to do after the training program is generally a mystery. The first step—defining exactly what we expect the supervisors to do with regard to employee relations—is often missing. Instead of training supervisors in the traditional, abstract, fuzzy "motivation and leadership" nonsense, which is difficult to put into actual on-the-job practice, the effort should be directed to coaching supervisors on *performance expectations*.

If we are successful in clarifying specific expectations for supervisory behavior toward supervisees and in coaching them on a continual basis to ensure that those expectations are met, everyone wins. What this means is that managers must model for supervisors the behavior they expect supervisors to have with supervisees. This is simple and logical and contrary to the traditional "send 'em to a training program, but don't expect me to go" attitude. Managers can model the appropriate behavior for the supervisors, who are then trained to set performance expectations for their people and to coach individuals to improve performance. This is what managers and supervisors are *paid* to do. Successful coaches/managers (1) determine a game plan for each team, (2) set and communicate expectations with each team player, (3) coach to achieve those expectations, (4) correct problems as they arise, (5) frequently give positive, specific feedback and (6) formally appraise performance.

Crucial Assumptions

This model assumes that a systematic approach is more likely to be successful than random hit-or-miss training done in a vacuum. It assumes that managers must be models for supervisors if supervisors are to be models for their people. It further assumes that the employee relations policies are appropriate to the people and environment and are systematic: a "no-fault" attendance policy rather than "excused/unexcused", a guaranteed four-step correction procedure, and so on. This model also assumes that performance expectations/ standards for each different job can only be determined by the persons in that job and their immediate supervisor or manager, *not* by Human Resources, Corporate or outside consultants.

The model also assumes that although you can train supervisors in the *process* of setting performance expectations, only they can determine *content*. *Performance coaching* by the supervisor is assumed to go on daily with periodic *performance appraisals*. And a final assumption—that everything will be put in writing, with both parties (the supervisor and the supervisee) signing the "agreement" so each person knows exactly what he or she has "contracted" to do.

Getting Started

Many managers agree that the "state of the art" of supervisor training is miserable. Most agree that performance expectations/standards and appraisals are basically useless. As a first step, management must sit down with each supervisor and mutually agree upon a clear list of performance expectations that can be behaviorally measured (no traits such as loyalty, trustworthiness, kindness, obedience, cheerfulness). Then observe the supervisor's behavior and, as needed, clarify expectations, offer guidance, and identify training needs.

Summary and Key Points

Encouraging employees' participation in determining the content of their work is an additional effort that can be made to improve the job satisfaction, motivation, and productivity to the workforce, and it is a useful adjunct to efforts to maintain unionfree status.

The impact of this participation and involvement on supervision is perhaps the most outstanding effect. As has been said many times, the first-line supervisor is the key to productivity as well as to the maintenance of unionfree status. The participation of employee groups in problem-solving and goal-setting activities changes the supervisor's role, and in most cases, it is a change for the better.

In addition to the changes in job content possible through job redesign, the mere fact of having been consulted often has resulted in an important change in a positive direction in employee attitudes. Consultation signifies that management has confidence in people and raises the degree of trust present in the work environment.

Furthermore, due to the differences in value systems, as described in chapter 6, the matching of employees with jobs is critical to job satisfaction. Because of the difficulty of changing employee values and redesigning jobs, one of the most outstanding opportunities lies in assigning people to jobs that are meaningful from their point of view. Selection and placement, therefore, not only at the point of hire but later in the person's advancement and movement in the corporation, provides an opportunity for motivating people and increasing their pro-company attitudes.

People do not organize against themselves. When they feel alienated from their work, they feel alienated from the corporation. When supervisors feel alienated from the corporation, they also feel alienated from their role and from the employees who report to them. Not all people need, require, or prefer a meaningful "enriched" job, but the opportunity to participate, whether or not the opportunity is utilized, signifies the concern of management for the potential of human beings to make a contribution to the success of the enterprise. Management value systems may set the goals of the organization, but the value systems of the people within them may give expression to problem-solving and goal-setting techniques. Not only does this result in improvements in productivity in a majority of cases, it has additional impact on morale, attitudes, and the employees' desire to organize to prevent the corporation from restricting their jobs or their opportunity to have a meaningful existence at work.

CHAPTER 9

MANAGEMENT SYSTEMS AND PROCEDURES

The systems and procedures used to operate the organization are often designed completely by management, from management's viewpoint of what is necessary to operate the organization effectively. There is, however, an opportunity for employees to participate in designing the means of achieving productivity. The improvements that employees can effect in the operation of the organization are limited only by the opportunities they have to participate. Although not all people, given their value systems, may make a meaningful contribution, having the opportunity to do so signifies to them that management is concerned with the employees as individual human beings. Systems and procedures, including the policies, procedures, and work rules that are necessary in every organization, have impact on morale, attitudes, and productivity. It is necessary to design the systems and procedures of the corporation—not only those concerning the work, but those affecting the environment—in such a way that it is possible for employees to do a good job and to feel good about themselves as well as the corporation they work for.

Involvement in Design

Why should management involve employees in the design of systems and procedures? The answer is relatively simple. Without involvement, people will show their creativity in subverting the best-designed systems and procedures that management establishes for the accomplishment of work and the administration of procedures. On the other hand, groups of employees, when given the opportunity, can make meaningful contributions to the improvement of the efficiency of administrative practices. For example, many computerized policies and procedures are unfit for human consumption. A great majority of these have been designed to satisfy the needs of the computer rather than the needs of the people who must operate within the restrictions imposed by the type of input and output that the computer requires. People therefore use their creativity to devise methods for working around computer systems so that the needs of human beings rather than machines are satisfied. Given the challenge and opportunity, however, employee groups and ad hoc committees can often improve the efficiency of even the apparently best-designed management systems and practices. How many times have accounting procedures, purchasing policies, and attendance rules been successfully avoided by creative employee groups? There are innumerable opportunities for management to involve people in creative problem-solving and goal-setting in the area of employee relations policies. For example, it is extremely difficult for external consultants to management and the human resources department to design a pension program that is meaningful to the rank-and-file employees. This is true for a very simple reason: Consultants, top management, and human resources professionals are not rank-and-file employees. It has been shown in more than one organization that employee groups can make a meaningful contribution to the design of pension programs and other benefits.

The management that does not permit the involvement of people in the design of systems and procedures for the administration of the organization is forgetting the simple fact that people *do* participate in the impact that these systems have on the organization. Here again, the use of ad hoc committees can have a powerful impact on the efficiency with which systems and procedures are designed, so that they are not only acceptable to both management and the workforce, but create more efficient administrative procedures.

Consistency in Administration

Without consistency in administration by supervisory personnel, the best-designed policies and procedures are of little avail in maintaining unionfree status. It has been shown many times that consistent application of a stringent rule has more positive impact on employees than the arbitrary, capricious application of a reasonable rule. Consistency in administration of management systems and procedures is a function of supervisory training, attitude survey feedback, and the policy itself. Some policies and practices may be formulated in such a way that it is impossible to administer them in a consistent, fair, and honest manner. Administrative consistency is achieved by several factors: Feedback from the employee group, the design of the procedure, and the effectiveness with which people can operate under the policy or procedure.

Attendance is a good example of an employee relations concern in which consistency is essential. Unfortunately, the attendance policies of most organizations allow managers and supervisors to be consistently inconsistent.

An attendance policy which is vague or fails to set guidelines for supervisors and supervisees obviously provides opportunities for favoritism and discrimination. Of numerous handbooks from a cross-section of organizations, only a few had clear guidelines on *expectations* for attendance, or conversely, absenteeism. When consulting with organizations, we find that only rarely will the supervisors of a company state the same attendance guideline. When the human resources manager is queried, the usual response is, "We leave it up to our managers and supervisors to determine what is excessive absenteeism." It is no surprise that no two agree on what is excessive.

The practice of *excused vs. unexcused* reasons for an absence compounds the consistency problem. The excused/unexcused policy requires that each supervisor practice medicine, dentistry, child psychology, automotive diagnostics and weather forecasting. This policy consumes immeasurable energy by encouraging creative excuses, it buys a lot of Mercedes for lawyers, and it gives a warm feeling to union organizers. It also drives most supervisors crazy.

The principle of consistency can only be applied when there are no excused absences and the guideline for the amount of scheduled work time expected is uniform for all employees. A *no-fault attendance policy* not only meets these two requirements, but also gives Title VII protection and can be easily communicated and administered. A no-fault attendance policy specifies the amount of *scheduled* time expected to be worked (or conversely, the amount of time permitted for absence) for all employees—both office and production. As long as any individual remains within the guidelines, no questions about any absence are asked and no reasons are solicited. (Of course, time which is not *scheduled* to be worked is not counted if the person is absent, e.g. benefit paid absences or hospitalization.) There are no excused absences, period.

There are some who say that such a system of attendance control is too strict, and they cite possible rare events or individual hardship cases. Most of these relate to health, or rather the lack of health. But these unfortunate situations fall under Leaves of Absence, and the benefit plans of the organization or state laws provide rules and supplemental income. These are not the employee relations issues that disturb the consistency doctrine; it is the everyday, unconscious inconsistency that erodes morale and creates real or perceived favoritism. A no-fault attendance policy is not designed to handle the *exceptions*–its purpose is to clarify the everyday roles and rules for supervisors and supervisees.

The consistent application of a specific rule such as a no-fault attendance policy should not be viewed as limiting human freedom. *Au contraire,* it is the absence of reasonable rules by which to live that limits personal freedom. In the absence of rules, inconsistencies arise. The mutually shared guidelines of any group—large or small—prevent chaos and anarchy and permit human freedom to flourish *within those rules.* (Self-Audit 6, on consistency in administration of work rules, is in Appendix A.)

Symbols and Emotion

Some systems and procedures are more important for their symbolic impact and the emotional response of the employees than they are for the policy itself. For example, one of the most symbolic elements of working life today is the time clock, which symbolizes the difference between salaried and hourly people in a company. Other symbolic impacts come from job titles, such as hourly and salaried, white-collar and blue-collar, and management and labor, all of which indicate the "haves" and "have nots."

The value systems of individuals and different employee groups are important in the understanding of symbols and emotion. A careful reconsideration and analysis of the value systems concept described in Chapter 7 will give a great deal of insight into the systems and procedures that are not appropriate to employee belief patterns.

For example, systems and procedures should be maintained at a relatively noncomplex level for people with the tribalistic value system. Their systems and procedures should come from management, and management for them is the immediate supervisor—the beginning and the end of the entire management process.

Systems and procedures are most readily compatible with a conformist value system. People with conformist values place a high degree of relevance on consistency of administration and a great belief in the right of management to determine what should be done in their work. People with the manipulative value system, on the other hand, may prepare systems and procedures for other people to follow, but they themselves prefer a great deal of latitude in the execution of their job and the attainment of their personal and organizational objectives. Those with a sociocentric value system believe that systems and procedures rigidify society and are incumbrances to human relationships.

The Importance of "Why"

Perhaps more important than the clarity of systems and procedures in and of themselves is the opportunity for employees to understand why the policies are as they are. It is a rare occasion when procedure manuals or employee handbooks define why a particular policy or practice exists, much less its relevance to the employee's own personal employment relationship. Perhaps this is because many management policies and practices have no particular reason for existence except the perpetuation of tradition. Oral or written communications of management systems and procedures, therefore, should include a clear discussion of why the policy exists and its importance to the organization and to the individual in the execution of his or her job, the maintenance of the organizational structure, and the attainment of organization objectives.

Summary and Key Points

All organizations have processes and procedures; they are a necessary attribute to the organizational structure. Avoiding overcomplication of systems and procedures, however, is a critical factor in the maintenance of unionfree status. They should be maintained in as simple a form as possible, be as few in number as possible and be capable of consistency in administration. The symbolic and emotional aspect of systems and procedures depends on the value systems of the individual employee. As long as managers recognize that the belief patterns of various employee groups may differ widely from their own, they will recognize that systems and procedures must be designed with the user and recipient of the system in mind. The involvement of employee groups and ad hoc committees in the design of management systems and procedures is a meaningful methodology for the design of systems and procedures. It not only helps hold the organization together, but helps rather than hinders individual employees in doing their jobs effectively, and enhances pride in the organization.

CHAPTER 10

GROWTH OPPORTUNITY AND ADVANCEMENT

Depending on their value systems, people find personal growth meaningful or meaningless. Advancement in status in the hierarchy and pay and job grades also are meaningful to some employees but not to others. The managerial value system prescribes that all individuals should be developing themselves and moving forward to upper levels of the organizational hierarchy. Some of the value systems, such as tribalistic and conformist, either are uninterested in personal advancement and growth or else leave this to management to determine. Other systems, such as those of the manipulative and existential groups, define personal growth and advancement as one of the key motivational aspects of work. With due consideration to the value systems of employees, the opportunities for advancement must be present, regardless of whether individual employees choose to use them.

One of the key ingredients in the maintenance of unionfree status is the provision to the present workforce of opportunities for growth and advancement. This is generally known as "promotion from within." Whenever individuals are hired into the organizational structure from outside, with a resulting bypassing of present employees, a great deal of dissatisfaction generally occurs, even though some of the people bypassed may not be interested in the job openings themselves. Promotion from within is generally followed in unionfree companies. In unionized organizations, the opportunities for advancement are generally limited to the immediate task or the next job up in the organizational hierarchy.

Promotion-from-within policies, therefore, are essential to maintaining unionfree status; however, they must be properly administered with clarity and believability from the viewpoint of the people affected. In general practice, unionfree companies promote on the basis of merit to the greatest extent possible. A unionized company usually operates on the basis of seniority; promotion for unionfree companies generally depends on the judgment of supervisors and management in the selection of the individuals who will move up in the organizational hierarchy. The organization that wishes to maintain unionfree status, therefore, should implement a promotion-from-within policy, preferably on the basis of the capabilities of the individual, as demonstrated by prior job performance. When this is not feasible, the seniority factor should be given greater weight.

When we provide opportunities for the present workforce to begin gaining advantages economically and in terms of status, we have introduced a major deterrent to unionization.

Open Job Posting and Bidding

So you want the best qualified person for the job. That's good. Nearly every manager we talk to says that. But "wanting" the best qualified person isn't good enough—you have to be able to convert this goal into behavior. And, if you "want" to foster positive employee relations at the same time, you pretty much have to adopt a promote-from-within policy. The only promotion system that allows you to select the best qualified person for the job while promoting from within is the job bidding/posting system.

The theory behind job posting/bidding is that people should be able to find jobs inside the organization as easily as they can find jobs at other companies. The original reason job posting evolved is that qualified people, unaware of jobs available within the organization, were leaving to take the same kinds of jobs with other organizations. Tired of unnecessarily losing good people to other companies and suffering recurring recruitment and training costs, a few enlightened managers decided to make available jobs more visible to existing employees by posting them.

When a manager wishes to fill a job opening, the natural thing to do is search his or her own territory to find a candidate who meets the job specifications. If someone is found, the individual will be transferred to the new job (sometimes involuntarily). If an appropriate candidate is not readily available, the next logical step is contacting other managers to see whether someone in their departments is available for the job opportunity. Given no suitable candidates, the human resources department might be called in. When all internal sources fail, an advertisement would be placed in the "Help Wanted" columns of newspapers. The advertisement would briefly outline the opportunity available; experience and education required; where the job is located; and, possibly, the compensation offered.

This is the means of filling openings in many organizations when there is no immediately available candidate within sight. The results of the help wanted advertisement may yield a suitable prospect who will be made an offer to leave her or his present organization and join the new one. After the job is filled from outside, present employees often complain that some of them were at least equally qualified. In more than one organization, people have been hired in one door to replace those with like skills who are leaving by another door because the available job opportunities were not evident to them before they elected to terminate.

Some computer-oriented organizations have attempted to establish the corporate version of the "dating bureau" by storing job requirements in the memory bank and matching these to the individual employee's attributes. Skills inventory systems occasionally do work; however, they have problems with data obsolescence and sorting and matching parameters. A number of organizations have attempted to operate skills inventories, then abandoned them as expensive card-shuffling routines, with human beings inadequately captured as magnetic images in a tape reel. Skills inventories, in general, have failed to fill the bill, either for the organization or for the employees.

The open and free job market concept has the advantage of coupling real-time data of people with on-line requirements from a manager. As long as the best candidates are available within the manager's own operation, it will not be necessary to provide either skills inventories or open job markets. These conditions rarely exist. Employees do terminate to seek opportunities elsewhere when those opportunities are, in fact, available within their present company. Why not adapt the external and open market system to the internal operations of the corporation?

This is, in fact, what some organizations have done and many are considering. They are creating policies and procedures to operate a system for job opportunity modeled after the free market system—that is, job posting and bidding. The organizations that have established, or are setting up, job posting and bidding systems do not do this for altruistic reasons, or only as a means of alleviating a turnover or morale problem. Rather, the investment in employees requires the retention of skills to reduce the cost of turnover replacement. Furthermore, if the organization intends to grow and to follow a promotion-from-within policy, then any mechanism for facilitating internal promotion and career advancement is worth consideration.

Basic Design Features

In its simplest form, job posting and bidding is the corporate version of the public system. It features a "Help Wanted" column and voluntary résumés. These first two steps are followed by an interview assessment, with a job offer and/or rejection. There is no requirement that the human resources department act as an employment agency; individual employees are on their own to initiate a response to a job posted on the bulletin board or published in the employee newspaper. There is an additional virtue: It is cost effective. A computerized data base is not mandatory, although machine records may be useful in very large organizations. A significant advantage is the freshness of the data, since they are created anew each time. Managers and supervisors wishing to survey the organization for someone who is qualified conduct their posting as if they were going to use *The New York Times* or the *Chicago Tribune*. Then the normal course of events follows (with both the advantages and disadvantages of the external system).

Enlightenment or Permissiveness?

Is an open posting and bidding system an invitation to excessive employee permissiveness, or is it an enlightened form of self-reallocation of employees in the workforce? Will some employees attempt to take advantage of the organization by hopping from job to job internally, just as they might skip from corporation to corporation, seeking only their own advantage and betterment and not staying long enough to make a contribution? Is it not management's prerogative to place employees where they will be most productive? There are many other practical questions.

In the author's experience in the design and operation of such systems, some answers have appeared. Most organizations have entered into job posting and bidding systems because of turnover and employee complaints that it is difficult to find out what jobs are open elsewhere in the corporation. Some managers may be threatened by the idea that employees can change from job to job and department to department without actually leaving the corporation. Some of these managers *should* have high anxiety if people are given the freedom to change to a new job or new department without actually leaving and forfeiting their seniority rights and benefits. Job posting and bidding makes it easy for employees to change jobs without breaking the "inertia" that causes people to stay. It is disconcerting to a manager with a need to control, who uses job security as a threat to influence the workforce. (Low turnover may be a sign of severe problem-people staying for the wrong reasons). Complete management control over career patterns and advancement may once have been acceptable, but no more. Some organizations are reluctant to initiate open job posting and bidding because of concern that employees will pursue escapism, moving from department to department to avoid unpleasant situations that are not so unsettling as to cause them to quit.

Most of the objections to open job posting and bidding systems originate from a deep-felt need of managers to control "the situation" and protect themselves from encroachment on their management prerogatives (whatever that comprehends). But, the needs of the managers should not override the establishment of a job posting and bidding system. The needs of individuals and the organization, rather than those of any manager *per se*, should determine and control the process and policies on open job posting and bidding systems. The advantages to the corporation of the internal free market system appear to far outweigh the disadvantages to any individual department or manager. As the expectations of employees increase, in terms of their mobility from corporation to corporation and the portability of fringe benefits, the same kinds of expectations will be directed toward the corporation itself.

Who Participates

What about the organization with distinct functions? If the skills of the people are applicable to only one department, does posting and bidding make sense? Probably the answer is "no." These organizations will lose people to another corporation in spite of any attempts to tie on the "golden handcuffs" or provide real or fictional advancement opportunities.

The question of whether to post all jobs or to restrict posting to managerial or professional jobs is primarily a matter of policy. However, that policy will be shaped by the basic character of the organization, which determines whether or not the people are treated as distinct classifications or as equal members of the organization. In a few corporations, job posting is limited to professional classifications because of the presence of a labor union, which restricts the posting and bidding system. In unionized companies, posting and bidding systems are generally seniority-based, which is contrary to the basic philosophy of the open job system, where the most qualified person gets the opportunity. However, it is understandable that most labor unions use seniority-related systems, since management too often has shown favoritism and excluded people from promotion for reasons other than merit.

It is characteristic for professionals to seek out opportunities for further advancement through their own initiative. However, this is not always a function of the attributes of professionals as personalities; it could reflect the lack of opportunities for people in the blue-collar ranks to move upward. Most professionals are accustomed to pursuing career advancement through their own initiative by seeking job opportunities either internally or externally. The posting of jobs within the corporation according to skill attributes and advancement opportunities will be somewhat more natural for those with professional or advanced education. Employees who are accustomed to working with professionals will also find the posting and bidding system natural. High-skill drafters, electronic technicians, machinists, toolmakers, secretaries, computer operators and others will be able to adopt readily to a job-posting system, since it is a pattern that is followed by professionals.

Although these basic motivation and personality attributes may apply to some of the lower-skilled blue-collar workers, it is more the exception than the rule. This is not to detract from these individuals either as employees or human beings, but simply to recognize that the self-initiated pattern of career advancement is less characteristic. This does not mean that the blue-collar population should be excluded from open job posting and bidding; there will be a sufficient number of people in this group who will be interested. This is particularly true of those people who have entered the workforce at a low-skill level, but do have an intrinsic interest in advancement. These are the same blue-collar workers who find job enrichment meaningful.

Managers who create a posting system completely in their own image of self-determination and initiative are most likely to design a system in which only a small percentage of the population can participate. It will be necessary to provide systems, procedures, counseling, and other factors for a fair percentage of the workforce, to increase their probability of moving upward. It follows, therefore, that the design of the system would be best developed by the involvement of ad hoc employee committees. Committees composed of slices of all job grades and levels of the organization would then design the systems and procedures best suited for all employees.

The most appropriate time to post jobs is when the opportunity is still open to available employees, before any external market opportunities have been pursued. A period of one to two weeks is sufficient time for posting a job inside the corporation, prior to the time it is opened to the public. This provides enough opportunity for present employees to check postings, either in the company newspaper or on the bulletin board, and file an application.

If there are no suitable candidates inside the corporation, there should be no pressure on the manager to accept unqualified employees. When no qualified candidates come forward through the bidding process, the manager may pursue the external market. The primary reason for starting open job posting and bidding systems is to give qualified candidates the first opportunity to move forward within the corporation. If there are none, then it is logical to proceed to the external market. As a precaution, however, one should be always mindful of the Equal Employment Opportunity Commission and Title VII of the Civil Rights Act to assure that the system is not causing employees to file charges of discrimination.

Should an employee inform her or his present supervisor about looking for another job inside the company? Following the job market theory, it would not be necessary to discuss that intention with the present boss. Some companies using job posting and bidding do require prior knowledge of the supervisor. Others simply require that the present supervisor be informed prior to an actual interview with a new manager; that is, it is confidential until there is a reasonable interest. In other instances there is no requirement that the present supervisor be informed at all, until the individual employee has actually accepted an offer to transfer. At that time the employee gives notice that he or she is moving to another department and has, in fact, accepted an opportunity there.

In the typical job posting and bidding situation, four to six weeks' notice to the present boss is generally required before transfer can take place. In a number of companies, the employee may be held for longer periods of time if an immediate transfer would create an extreme hardship for the organization that she or he is leaving. These cases generally require higher-level management review, possibly at an officer level, to assure that the request to retain the employee is realistic. In such cases, the new job may have to be held open.

It is probably more important in the internal job market that individual employees be informed of the reasons for not having been selected than it is in the external market. Particularly critical at this stage are the Equal Employment Opportunity regulations. Equally important is communication to internal bidders who are turned down in favor of a newly hired employee. Here, the potential employee relations damage is great. Feedback may come directly to the bidder from the manager or it may flow through the human resources department. In either case, it is necessary to provide honest feedback. Remedial measures to qualify the employee for the next job opening (training, education, or experience) should be suggested. If the performance appraisal process in the company is full of noise, rather than clear signals, the job posting and bidding system may help bring to the surface some situations that will require major policy changes. These will not be the fault of the job posting system, but rather the fact that job posting systems tend to bring many employee relations problems to light.

There are some circumstances in which jobs should not be posted. Jobs that are clear ladders of progression and are primarily based on experience within a single function, or a single department, do not need to be posted. However, the purpose of job posting is to seek a spectrum of candidates across the organization when the necessary skills and requisites are not clearly evident, just as the open market requires. Entry-level jobs that require specific academic or professional training may not be posted, unless there is a possibility that an hourly individual could become salaried. In other words, it makes no sense to post jobs when it is completely unreasonable for an employee to move ahead. It may make no sense to post entry-level unskilled jobs, except for purposes of publicity and referrals of friends by employees. The same may be true of many jobs filled by college recruiting. In these cases, we should assure ourselves that a college education is really relevant to the performance of the jobs.

Jobs at department, division, or vice-presidential level conceivably could be posted. Whether or not they *should* be posted is a matter of practical reality. Does the organization, in fact, know enough about the employees near the top of the pyramid to be able to select candidates for key managerial positions without having to place internal or external advertisements? Probably not, unless the top of the pyramid is sufficiently small so that all potential candidates are well known. If there is any possibility that the organization may have to go external and place public ads or seek professional management recruiting assistance, then internal job posting may be quite realistic at the division or vice-presidential level.

For a number of reasons, it is useful for the human resources department to serve as a clearing house, counselor, and go-between. First of all, this assists the receiving manager, because they can screen out unqualified candidates. Human Resources may be able to help people understand why their bids are not realistic. Those who appear qualified pass through to the manager for screening and interviewing. Since there is always the possibility that real or alleged discrimination may occur, the involvement of Human Resources is a realistic addition to the process. The job opportunity approach needs monitoring also, due to the tendency of some managers to subvert the system. The most frequent manipulative technique is to preselect a candidate, then to go through the motions of posting and interviewing. When this is discovered (as it will invariably be), there can be a great deal of difficulty in relations with employees. Perhaps there is no more detrimental or dangerous aspect of the system than such violations of policies and procedures. This should not be permitted under any circumstances; it will completely undermine the basic concepts. (One company that is using job-posting procedures has an interesting technique for dealing with a manager who violates the system: They post the name).

Job Classifications. Without adequate and up-to-date job classifications, job-posting systems cannot work well. Of course, inadequate job slotting will hurt the organization whether the posting system exists or not. The main difference is the visibility of the posted job grade and pay structure: With posting, any inadequacies or inequities in rate structure and job grades will be clearly evident to all employees. Prior to the implementation of the job-posting system, it is necessary to ensure that the compensation structure is in shape and up-to-date. This is another reason that the Human Resource department's involvement can be quite helpful.

If employees are able to analyze the wage and salary structure, will this not cause employees to critically evaluate the pay system? The answer to this very pointed question is broader than the posting and bidding of jobs. It involves the basic philosophy of the company on job grades and rate changes. If the job grade structure and rate ranges are in line and competitive, then there should be nothing to hide; in fact, the posting of grades and rates will probably give a significant incentive to keep the structure up-to-date and equitable. From the individual employee viewpoint, it is difficult to determine whether some jobs are lateral or upward movements in the career path; therefore, at a minimum, disclosure of the job grade structure is necessary.

In some companies, an individual can place a "position wanted" ad. This has been done in company posting and bidding systems with a very high yield. As many as half of those placing "position wanted" ads find the position that they are seeking. Their postings may be kept anonymous by channeling them through Human Resources to provide a "front" for the individual.

Controls on Bidding

In job-posting systems, there is a wide range in the percentage of bids to actual promotions. This may be a function of the number of truly qualified candidates, or it may simply reflect the specifications on the jobs posted. Postings for jobs need to be written precisely to avoid giving unrealistic expectations to employees and flooding the system with paperwork. Ratios of ten-to-one are not unusual, but precision posting should bring this number down to one out of four. This is also affected by job-progression lines. Some jobs have many paths toward them, which permits and realistically encourages a large number of people to bid for a single opening.

It is necessary to limit the number of bids that an employee may make at one time, usually to two. This prevents employees from broadcasting résumés and overwhelming the system. Feedback and counseling are required for individuals who feel it necessary to bid for many jobs, particularly jobs that are alien to their skill or experience.

After five or six unsuccessful bids, it is appropriate to ask the individual to come to Human Resources for help with "career counseling." Remedial training or additional education is often an answer. A tactical move from the present position to an intermediate position to gain experience may be advisable, and a person can be helped to map out a longer-term career plan instead of simply bidding repeatedly. Career counseling is a worthwhile function if it is professionally staffed and operated. With posting and bidding systems, the need for counseling is not increased, but it is more clearly manifested. In addition to career counseling, employee education through seminars or printed media in how to bid and how to conduct oneself in an interview is useful.

The receiving manager is best qualified and certainly has the responsibility for selecting staff from the outside, and should have the same responsibility on internal transfers and promotions. The manager should not be under any pressure to take an employee who is unqualified. Employees who are marginal in performance should not be permitted to transfer without the express approval and understanding of the receiving manager and the human resources operation. Otherwise there may be a number of employees who drift from job to job internally, just as they float from job to job in the external market. Some organizations place restrictions on transfers so employees with unsatisfactory performance ratings or disciplinary status are not permitted to move. The manager who receives the employee has to be in a position to have full knowledge and control and make the final decision. Of course, it is the employee's ultimate decision as to whether or not to accept an offer to move, just as it is in the external market.

It is a matter of policy whether present supervisors should be informed of all active bids before their completion. If there is full knowledge on the part of the employee and the potential new manager, then discussion with the present supervisor is reasonable. If this is done, the employee must have full knowledge that the present supervisor is being contacted, just as is done in the external job market.

The function of training and education becomes much clearer under job-posting and bidding systems. Training and education are resources and means to the end of career movement, rather than ends in themselves. In other words, the provision of training media becomes a critical necessity in the job-posting system, because it is an investment in people. Training and education may also be approached from a return on investment viewpoint: Additional investment in human beings is expected to yield a return through the high productivity and performance of experienced employees. The return on investment must be greater than the cost of turnover replacement. Since it has been shown that some employees stay not because they *want* to stay, but because they *have* to stay, the opportunity for education and training as an adjunct to job posting and bidding is a reasonable step to assure continuity. This is particularly true of low-skill blue-collar employees, who are more likely to stay in jobs and with companies when they really do not want to do so, but are required to do so because of the economics involved in changing jobs. With reality-oriented career counseling, the return on investment in education and training can be quite high and provide greater cost effectiveness and cost control over education and training than is present in most organizations. These functions become more a career-development opportunity than a fringe benefit.

The upgrading of present employees will, in the long run, produce a more stable workforce and help cope with the problem of rising turnover and job mobility. The answer is in the degree of goal-directedness of the career path the individual has mapped. The more effective the career-development strategy, the better the return on investment. Posting and bidding without a clear goal path is not only wasteful, but also may create expectations that increase employee dissatisfaction.

When used with integrity, a job posting/bidding system can have tremendous long-term positive impact on employee attitudes. This impact is so beneficial that most organizations using the system post jobs *even when no qualified candidates are expected to be found.* There are three reasons for this: (1) an unknown, qualified candidate just might step forward; (2) there is no downside risk to posting the job; and (3) most people would rather read about the opening on a company bulletin board than in the local newspaper.

The three biggest problems with job posting/bidding are pre-selection of candidates, shifting qualifications, and poor feedback. Managers who pre-select a candidate before the job is posted and all qualified bidders have been interviewed undermine the system's integrity as well as their own. The repercussions in terms of employee attitudes are so negative that we staunchly recommend that any manager guilty of pre-selection be hung by his thumbs from the company flagpole.

Qualifications which "shift" after they are posted also undermine the integrity of the system. Careful thought and consideration of qualifications must be given to each job *prior* to posting. If the job description and qualifications are accurate when posted, you won't have charges of favoritism or discrimination resulting from subsequent changes in qualification requirements or scores of people bidding for every job.

The only person who should give initial feedback to unsuccessful candidates is *the supervisor or manager who does the interviewing and makes the final decision.* This responsibility should *never* be delegated to anyone else. All candidates must receive honest, candid feedback as well as guidance on how to prepare to be better qualified for the next opening. Flippant or ambiguous explanations to unsuccessful candidates cripple the system and can cause turnover of good employees.

Summary

Organizations must grow in order to survive and continue to have a meaningful existence. So must individuals, both as employees and as human beings. The organization grows through the acquisition of resources—physical and human assets. It expects a reasonable return on its physical as well as its human resources. Capital and physical resources that are underutilized produce a poor return on investment. The same is true for human resources.

The underutilization of human talent, blocked in jobs below effective skill and experience levels, fails to make a suitable contribution to the organization and to the individual. This produces a low return on investment as well as a low "return on self." Low turnover may be a manifestation of high job satisfaction or simply the result of high inertia and immobility. It is particularly detrimental to the organization to lose the people who could make a significant contribution but who leave because they are unable to find out what jobs are open elsewhere in the corporation. Skills inventories and other management selection devices fail to work as efficiently and effectively as the external open job market. The creation of the corporate version of the open job market makes it possible for employees to seek career paths while remaining in the corporation. Avoiding underutilization of human talent is critical, particularly when viewed in the light of the slow rise of productivity versus the high rate of climb of wages.

Open job posting and bidding may challenge some traditional management policies and prerogatives; however, it is consistent with the value systems of increasing numbers of employees. The charting of their own paths through life and career in the corporate maze is a meaningful experience to increasing numbers of people. Job posting and bidding is a means for people to obtain jobs that are motivating and satisfying and thereby place themselves in positions in which they are more productive. Individuals who are "maze-bright" have accomplished this inside or outside the corporation. The provision of a facilitating mechanism such as job posting and bidding makes it legitimate for these employees to seek their end with their present employer. Individual self-selection into jobs is more likely to produce a good fit between an employee's motivation patterns, needs, and value system than a policy that gives the individual little choice. Job opportunities that suit the career path and life style of the individual may be provided internally just as naturally as they are provided externally. Providing the freedom and opportunity to self-select job choices internally should provide retention of employees for reasons of positive job satisfaction rather than simple retention in a state of dissatisfaction, indifference, or alienation.

Job posting is not a new fringe benefit. It is a meaningful self-regulating system for the reallocation of talent among the workforce within the corporation in the same pattern that is used naturally among organizations. The particular policies and procedures of an organization should be consistent with its overall philosophy toward people and its mechanisms and employee relations programs in other areas. We should seek the assistance of the employees themselves through ad hoc committees or the assistance of external advisors who have experienced job-posting systems. This may help custom-design the most appropriate system to fit the environment, rather than simply duplicating what has occurred elsewhere.

In any form, job posting and bidding is the most natural approach to employee selection and placement. This approach has been practiced in companies in Europe, Asia, and the United States, in large organizations as well as small, with professionals as well as skilled workers, and in a variety of organizational settings. Its ultimate payoff is improved return on human assets and increased job satisfaction.

The posting of available positions and required qualifications shifts the responsibility of moving up in the organization *onto the shoulders of individual employees rather than those of management.* Instead of having the "boss" or Human Resources determine who is ready for a promotion, an individual determines if and when he or she wants to move up by expressing an interest through a job bid. People who want to move up must prepare to meet qualifications and then take action and bid; they can no longer assert that they've been "passed over" without serious consideration.

Education and Training

Even though promotion from within and open job-posting and bidding systems are in existence, they may provide opportunities that individuals cannot utilize. The provision of education and training resources can enable many people to take advantage of a promotion-from-within policy and utilize the posting and bidding systems. However, a great deal of education and training is offered more as a fringe benefit than as an opportunity for growth, advancement, and higher compensation levels. Education is often perceived and offered as a panacea for the ills of employee morale. In fact, providing education and training resources without related opportunities to move forward and utilize those skills is not only a waste of economic resources but an invalidation of the company's policy.

It is the outcome of training and education that is most important, rather than the processes, techniques, or classroom hours. Education and training must be geared to the objectives of the organization and viewed as a return on investment. The concepts of management by objective are essential to the development of the education and training program. An organization may wish to provide general education as a fringe benefit program that is useful in and of itself. But if the program is described and offered as an opportunity to get ahead, when in fact there are no mechanisms for moving forward in the organization, the company has simply offered an opportunity for a decline in credibility and a rationale for desiring the seniority promotional opportunities that are generally found under union contracts.

Training and education can be provided on a relatively inexpensive basis. The costs of instruction, materials, instructors, and facilities are relatively low when compared with the cost of turnover, ineffective performance, scrap, and low productivity. Education and training can thus provide significant opportunities for an investment in people.

The return on investment will be realized as long as the program itself is designed with clear objectives in mind. Training without a purpose is a useless effort. It can have significant negative impact on attitudes, not only among rank-and-file employees but among supervisors who may have unrealistic expectations about what training can do for them and its effect on the employees they supervise.

Promote on Service or Performance?

One of the long-standing debates concerns the relative advantages and disadvantages of service and performance in promotion and growth opportunity. Service is the method preferred by most union memberships and union leaders. The reason for this is extremely simple: It is the case historically that many organizations have claimed to have a merit system but in fact have had a simple system of supervisor favoritism. Although the use of length of service is not necessarily the fairest methodology for determining advancement, it is at least easily understood and subject to little manipulation on the part of supervisory personnel.

There is one extremely important role in the application of merit programs: If a company wants to use performance as a basis for determining promotions, then there must be a logical, straightforward, well-understood system for judging and measuring who "merits" the opportunity. Here again is an opportunity for the involvement of employees in the design of systems and procedures. The judgment of merit according to various performance-review methodologies can be enhanced greatly by the use of ad hoc committees that will design a system acceptable to them and their supervisors. If the system is acceptable to the individuals involved, then it is by definition a good system, and it becomes another way of maintaining unionfree status.

Summary and Key Points

The opportunities to use collective activity decrease when growth opportunity and advancement are based on principles that permit and encourage individuals to move forward in the organization on the basis of their performance rather than their service within the group. The concept of promotion from within is critical to this, and it is followed by many more unionfree companies than union organizations. The use of a job-posting and bidding system holds significant promise, as long as it is well administered. Education and training are necessary to make the job-posting and bidding system work, so that promotion from within is realistically possible. Perhaps most important, the use of a merit system for determining advancement requires a valid and well-understood method of evaluating performance if it is to realize its full effectiveness as a program for maintaining unionfree status. Use our Self-Audit 7 on the issues discussed in this chapter. You'll find it in Appendix A.

CHAPTER 11

PAY AND BENEFITS

Although some unionfree companies pay significantly higher wages and provide much richer benefit programs for the employees than do union companies, by and large the less than 20 percent of the workforce that is unionized tends to enjoy about the same average wage rates and benefit programs. Unionfree corporations are not paying excessive wages and benefits. The way that pay and benefits are structured and administered is more important than the actual rates of pay. Compensation varies among industries; however, it is quite close within a single industry—whether the workforce is unionized or not.

One important factor that almost all unionfree companies fail to capitalize on is the effect of strikes, lockouts, and other work stoppages that frequently occur in unionized corporations. When wages are treated on a rate-per-hour basis, the average rates per hour in unionized companies are no longer ahead of unionfree companies in a given industry or community. The results of even a relatively short strike can offset the wage increases gained as a result of strikes and contract renegotiation. When these factors are taken into account on a long-range basis, many more unionfree companies move into the category of paying a higher average rate than unionized companies. It is important, therefore, to stress the annual salary equivalent of hourly compensation, rather than dwelling on differences in cents per hour between union and unionfree companies.

Money Means Different Things to Different People

A review of employee value systems (Chapter 7) reveals that an entire workforce cannot be of one mind. Therefore, it is useful to consider the disparities in values when designing or redesigning pay systems.

Pay-plan designers must seek to change or adapt pay systems to the organization's predominant values. To say that all production workers are dominantly tribalistic is an overgeneralization. Likewise, all managers are not manipulatives and all maintenance workers are not conformists.

It is possible, however, that there is a tendency, through selection and placement processes, for certain groups to lean toward one or two of the value systems profiles. Additionally, whether the organization is manufacturing or service based will make a difference in the values mix. Such a mix tends to occur as part of a natural evolutionary process, unless it is done deliberately during hiring, placing, and promoting employees.

Because employees and managers do not possess the same value systems when it comes to the meaning of money and how it should be delivered, companies must use pay systems that work for the people they pay, not use the systems they prefer.

One method companies can use is an existential approach to pay. In this instance, existential means that one particular value system or preferred pay system won't be imposed on everyone. The pay-plan designers will act existentially and design pay systems that work with whatever value systems are present in the workforce.

Moreover, there will not be a corporate standard pay system. The value systems of the various segments of the organization will be considered by type of work and level in the structure. From there, a pay system that is appropriate for those groups of employees (or at least the majority) will be established.

The following examples offer a more definitive listing of perceived equity and inequity of pay for each of the value systems:

- Existential—equity is pay that is not a central personal issue; inequity is pay that is used as a reward or punishment.
- Sociocentric—equity is pay that is equal for all work; inequity is pay that singles out individuals.
- Manipulative—equity is pay that distinguishes high achievers; inequity is pay that is based on service and skills.
- Conformist—equity is pay that is based on service and skills; inequity is keeping unproductive people on the payroll.
- Egocentric—equity is more pay than others; inequity is pay based on favoritism.
- Tribalistic—equity is the same pay for the entire work group; inequity is pay that's used to motivate.

It should be clear from these disparate mindsets that many pay systems popular with managers, compensation directors and consultants will be ineffective, and perhaps even destructive, with groups possessing some other value systems. For example, merit pay for tribalistic people is inadvisable. To a large extent, merit pay also is inappropriate for those employees with conformist values.

Egocentrism and commission or piece rates may be compatible in theory, but egocentrics rarely are satisfied with pay, regardless of the amount. On the other hand, because everyone has wants, needs, and families to care for, sociocentrics like to have the janitor paid as much as the chief executive officer.

Although merit pay is understood and appreciated by manipulative people, they know that the real money comes from promotions and bonuses. Existentials, however, do not care what their pay systems are called or how they work. If they perceive a personal inequity, they will make sure everyone knows.

Preannounced Goals

In contrast to the jelly bean theory—the concept of reinforcing collective activity and, therefore, teaching people to join unions—the concept of preannounced goals is consistent with the maintenance of unionfree status. Having preannounced goals relative to pay and benefits tells the employees what the company's policy is and indicates that it will not be necessary to take collective action to form or join a union in order to receive higher pay or better benefits. Preannounced goals generally relate to comparative wage and benefit structures. The goals may be stated as average rates, as compared to national surveys of selected corporations. The companies and industries selected should be compatible with the type of business in which the corporation is engaged.

The concept of preannounced goals also presumes that the company is willing to commit itself to keep its pay and benefits competitive. The goals may be stated in percentiles or in ranges around the average rate range or in excess of it. The concept must be further defined in terms of variability in frequency and amount of pay increases. It is possible to vary both the magnitude of the increase and the intervals at which the increases are given, psychological research clearly indicates that one of these factors should be held constant while the other is varied. In other words, a corporation may give approximately the same amount of increases at varying intervals, or give pay increases on a regularly scheduled basis but vary the magnitude according to the performance of the individual and/or the change in the market price of the particular skill involved.

It is our opinion that the most effective as well as the most easily administered practice is to give pay increases on a regularly scheduled basis but vary their magnitude, either according to the judged and measured performance of individuals or according to the change in wage surveys for comparable industries. For the majority of people in blue-collar jobs, regularly scheduled pay increases in which the entire group is given approximately the same percentage increase is most satisfactory. The key, however, is whether the jelly bean theory comes into play. The regularly scheduled pay increase for a group or individual negates the jelly bean effect as long as the preannounced goals in terms of wage-rate comparability are met—whether or not the company can "afford it." Paying people properly according to predetermined objectives is a cost of doing business, and it is a factor that any company that wishes to maintain its unionfree status must take seriously into account. If wage increases are allegedly unaffordable, then management would be wiser to look to methods of improving productivity and output per work-hour—to participative problem-solving, goal-setting, and cost-reduction techniques—than it would be to hold back on wage increases that people have been promised. Preannounced goals in the area of wages and benefits are valueless unless the company lives up to them.

Preannounced goals can have a significant impact in the area of economic factors relating to employment. The company must decide its objectives relative to pay and benefit levels, then move these levels to the appropriate rate each and every time that the wage or benefit surveys give evidence that these factors have fallen behind the goals. In fact, it is possible to give an increase that sets wage and benefit levels ahead of the survey, since survey averages continue to move and the company's rates will gradually slip behind. This gives the management of the corporation the opportunity to announce wage and benefit increases that do in fact exceed the average of competition.

No Secrets

Pay rate ranges and how they are determined are among the best kept secrets in many unionfree organizations. Unionized organizations are required by contract to disclose rate ranges, so the managers of these facilities have no choice but to spell them out in detail. Unfortunately, many managers in unionfree companies apparently believe either that employees don't need to know or that disclosure of the process and the ranges will generate a barrage of difficult questions. The implicit assumption is that people are better off not knowing how their pay system works.

This assumption gets blown to smithereens during union organizing drives. Once the Teamsters or Local 925 show up with their versions of a pay survey and rate ranges (which are usually based on the most lucrative contracts across the country), management acts "on the advice of counsel" and scrambles to communicate how pay rates are determined by the survey process and the minimum and maximum of each rate range. But by this time, employee trust in management has plummeted, and employees are far less receptive to what they hear.

Employees *must* understand their pay system to have good attitudes about their pay. It is ridiculous to expect people to have blind faith in something they know little or nothing about, especially when it affects them so much.

Most organizations overwhelm employees with information about benefits. There are orientations, booklets, slide shows, videotapes, group meetings, benefit update newsletters, etc. to cover every conceivable benefit. Yet typically there is but one line or paragraph about the pay policy. "Our policy is to pay better than or equal to other well-managed companies for comparable work." Explicitly, this tells employees nothing.

Implicitly, it tells them, "that's all you deserve to know."

The potential consequences of failing to educate employees on surveys and pay ranges are manifold: people have to guess how their pay compares to that of other companies; they are forced to do their own limited-sample surveys; they make assumptions about the rate ranges for their own or other jobs within the organization, and, to rationalize the differences they find, they presume favoritism on the part of supervision and management. Because their information is limited, the perception of other organizations' pay rates may be skewed high or low. In addition, it is human nature to assume that if no one can or will explain something, there must be a problem with it.

By educating employees about their pay system, management gains employee confidence and trust. Organizations with fair pay systems only stand to benefit from communicating them to employees. Explaining how the pay survey process works and how learning curves and supply and demand affect pay rates makes it easier for employees to understand why pay rates and annual general increases in the rate ranges vary. Management can show how it pays for jobs within the organization for internal equity, and show how it pays in comparison to other organizations within the community for external equity. The mystery of the pay system is solved, and employees can factually decide whether their pay is fair.

Managers using pay systems that (1) have rate range overlaps that permit employees in higher graded jobs to earn considerably less than others in lower graded jobs, (2) have people in the same rate range earning significantly different rates because of imprecise performance standards, (3) are based on an unintelligible merit pay system (which characterizes about 90 percent of all merit systems), and (4) are tied in with a poor or nonexistent performance appraisal system *should* be terrified of explaining them to employees, but they should never be so foolish as to think employees aren't aware of these blatant problems.

A Process for Presenting Pay Survey Results

If pay rates don't make sense, the company must determine the problem and fix it. If necessary changes are not made, employees will have little confidence in management. If necessary changes are made, or if the existing system has integrity, employees should be told. Here is a good way to tell them.

1. Select other organizations within a 50-mile radius that are in a similar or related business. Prefer those whose jobs are similar to your company's in terms of content, skills and learning curves. Extend the survey radius only if necessary to get a representative sample of jobs.
2. Form a survey team of supervisors from your organization, including a sample of rank-and-file employees. The survey team should do the initial on-site inspection of each survey company to determine whether its jobs are comparable. Do not base rate comparisons solely on job titles—the same job title can mean five different jobs in five different organizations.
3. Get the true paid average (base rate only with no shift or overtime premiums) from the companies' payroll departments for each job identified as comparable in content, skills and learning curve. Convert the data base to the internal structure of your company using the arithmetic mean of all survey employees lumped together. Weigh the data by the number of employees in the other organizations.
4. Create a series of charts that show the composite of the data for the jobs in each pay classification. The chart for each pay class will

show the lowest rate from the survey companies for that set of jobs, the highest rate paid in the survey, the true average or arithmetic mean, and the rates along the continuum. Participating companies may be identified, but not their pay levels.

5. Management meets with all employees, department by department, to explain the selection of the organizations surveyed, the jobs looked at, and then the results compiled in step 4. The survey team should be identified for the audience and should assist the department head with the presentation. A human resources representative should be on hand to help answer questions.

6. Show how your organization's current rates compare to the survey companies' rates and announce the general increase for each rate range effective during the current pay period. Clarify whether your company policy is to lead/lag the average of the survey companies or pay higher or lower than the average.

7. Explain how each pay grade will move upward by the amount dictated by the survey and pay comparison policy, which means each grade might move up by a different amount depending on the supply and demand of skills within the survey radius. It is important to educate all employees on this point because companies that move all grades by the same percentage or flat rate per hour destroy internal equity by compressing or expanding the spread from highest to lowest rates.

8. Post all charts used in the presentation along with the minimum, progression steps and maximum for each pay class. List the names of survey team members so they can be consulted for explanations. Add the description of the survey process and how rates are determined to the handbook, and include copies of the charts used during presentations (omit the rates so the handbook does not have to be updated after every increase).

9. Repeat the survey process every six or twelve months. After a survey team has inspected a survey company, that company's rates can be updated by telephone or mail. Always maintain a fixed time schedule to make the process predictable.

10. Use this same process for exempt, nonexempt and hourly jobs.

Merit Pay & Automatic Progression

Before designing a pay system, it is necessary to understand clearly what the system is meant to accomplish. Historically, these plans have taken one of two directions. When conceptualizing pay systems, some managers have a system in mind that will provide incentives for increased productivity (quality and quantity). Other managers do not expect that from a pay system. Instead, they seek only to neutralize pay as an issue so the majority of employees perceive that their pay is fair. The primary manifestation of the former thinking is the so-called merit-pay system, while the latter typically leads to automatic progression for all employees.

Merit Pay

These systems are characterized by broad ranges, usually a 50 percent spread from bottom to top. In addition, they have simple structures with only a minimum, midpoint and maximum identified. Such progression points are misnomers, however, because the midpoint is actually the maximum, and the maximum is fiction for most employees.

Progression through the range is based on a bell-curve distribution of performance of incumbents, with salary increases corresponding to performance. A significant characteristic of such systems is that performance measurement is variable and assumes a wide variance in performance levels. Employees compete against each other, not against a predetermined standard.

Merit pay was created by and for people who operate primarily out of the manipulative value system. The inherent assumption is that money motivates people, and the objective is to use dollars to manipulate employee behavior or performance. This system is generally instituted across the board, yet only a relatively small percentage of the working population is primarily motivated by money. Merit pay may warm executive hearts, but it tends to scorch those of many other employees.

Merit pay systems demand that people be paid different rates. This fosters a "look out for number one" spirit instead of teamwork. How, then, does a corporation reward its superstars? By training or terminating the unacceptable performers who burn holes in the company wallet. The few truly outstanding people can be rewarded by a bonus from outside the basic pay system. In this way you can financially reward meritorious performance without having to tolerate unacceptable performance.

Automatic Progression

Such systems are structured more rigidly. The range from minimum to maximum typically is less than a 25 percent spread. Progression steps are identified clearly, and all employees, regardless of performance variables, receive the same increase. This system assumes no performance differences, and progression is a function of time served in the pay grade. All employees move to the maximum.

Which is better?

Given the two predominant goals of managers—to motivate performance and/or to eliminate unfavorable attitudes—it is more likely that automatic

Figure 1

Pay and Values Matrix

+ = Good Fit   0 = Neutral   − = Bad Fit

Values % work force*	Merit Progr.	Auto. Progr.	Individ. Bonus	Group Bonus	Service Premium	Versat. Prem.
Existential 10%	0	0	0	0	0	0
Sociocentric 10%	−	+	−	+	+	0
Manipulative 15%	+	−	+	−	−	+
Conformist 40%	−	+	0	+	+	+
Egocentric Nil%	+	−	+	−	−	−
Tribalistic 25%	−	+	−	+	+	0
Fitness as % of population	15%+ 10%0 75%−	75%+ 10%0 15%−	15%+ 50%0 35%−	75%+ 10%0 15%−	75%+ 10%0 15%−	55%+ 45%0 0%−

*Approximation of dominant value system only. Varies by occupation and other demographics.

progression will be accepted by most employees, which results in more favorable attitudes. As shown in Figure 1, only 15 percent of the workforce has value systems that conflict with automatic progression, while it is likely that 75 percent believe merit pay is unfair. What about management's goal to motivate performance?

Assuming pay systems can provide an incentive to move most employees to improve their performance, which of the two systems creates an environment to achieve this goal? The answer is neither one. Generally, it is assumed that a merit-pay system yields higher quantity and/or quality levels for the organization, but this remains an assumption without proof.

Some of the confusion derives from the fact that several studies have found that incentive pay systems (individual and group) often result in

Pay and Benefits

increased performance in areas on which the incentives are based. The data seem to indicate that a bounty must be put on any area in which management seeks improvement.

Experiences with individual piece rates and group gainsharing have shown that this approach can work because there's a clear standard—a direct and understood connection between performance and reward—and an easily calculable payout. The reward is based on objective, relevant measurements of the job. All of these characteristics are absent from typical merit-pay plans.

Since merit pay obviously is not the answer, and progression based on blind seniority may not fill the bill either perhaps it is time to consider performance for pay.

Performance for Pay

The ultimate objective of any pay system is perceived equity—perceived by the payee rather than by the payor. The system that best accomplishes this objective is "Performance for Pay," the opposite of the "Pay for Performance" merit system.

While the theory of merit pay—people should be paid different rates for different levels of performance—is perhaps sound, it is corrupted in practice to the point where there is little, if any, merit in merit pay.

Performance for Pay—our recommended alternative—uses automatic progression up the learning curve and has three essential components:

1. accurate, precise, easy-to-understand job standards
2. quality supervision and management
3. proper selection and placement of personnel

Designing a Pay System
Traditional Approach

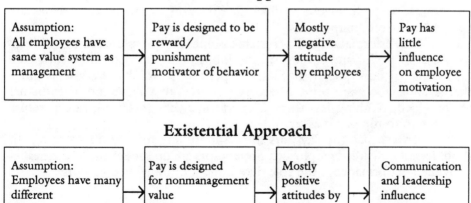

Existential Approach

If even one of these components is missing, the system will not work. The Performance for Pay system is like our three-legged stool—if one leg is missing, it cannot stand upright.

Precise job standards must be established for every job within the organization and then used to determine each job's individual learning curve. Each learning curve must then be divided into "steps." Once the job standards are set and the steps are established, a pay rate is set for each step. An employee who reaches that step, receives its specified rate of pay. Supervisors do not try to judge the relative merit of one person's performance to the group norm—they judge only whether an individual employee meets the eligibility standards for the next step increase.

Supervisors and managers are responsible for coaching and counseling employees up the learning curve, which means all must have excellent communication skills. Employees who fail to "step" up the learning curve receive positive corrective action from supervisors. Employees who don't progress up the learning curve within a specified time frame after coaching must either be placed in other jobs more compatible with their abilities or with another organization, and supervisors must be able to follow through with such action.

If job standards are precise; supervisors are well trained, experienced and responsible; and employees are selected on the basis of how well their skills, abilities and values match job requirements, the number of employees unable to "step" in their jobs will be quite small. Employees do not receive pay increases unless they progress to the next step in the learning curve. An employee who progresses up the learning curve faster than is expected, should be accelerated up the pay steps. This allows exceptional performers to more quickly reach the top of their rate ranges.

In a merit pay system, both performance and pay rates are variables. In this Performance for Pay system, pay is a constant, and performance is a variable until employees reach the top of the learning curve, when it too becomes a constant. People must either learn their jobs or find others more suitable to their abilities. There are no forced bell-shaped distribution curves or rank orderings, so every employee is free to earn top pay for top performance. Supervisors can concentrate on performance results rather than on arbitrary pay increases and person-to-person comparisons.

The Performance for Pay system assumes that people are responsible for their own behavior and success on the job. Employees determine their own rates of pay by how quickly they learn to perform their jobs. It is also assumed that training, tools and other necessary resources to achieve top performance are provided. Nothing less than top performance is tolerated, but in return progression to top pay is assured.

Performance for Pay puts the responsibility for pay increases on the shoulders of individual employees. Supervisors are no longer the "fall guys"—individual performance is the sole determinant of individual earnings.

Is Service Worth a Premium?

Even managers who are totally committed to Pay for Performance, and who oppose the idea of paying merely for years of service, feel comfortable with the practice of increasing benefits with seniority, perhaps because of a misguided belief in the theory of "total compensation"—the combined worth of pay and benefits. Managers of both unionfree and unionized organizations have embraced the compensation consultants' concept of a combined "package" of pay and benefits and have built their pay and benefit policies around it. Unfortunately, few managers or consultants have openly acknowledged that most employees—exempt, nonexempt and hourly—clearly separate pay and benefits. Regardless of how you intertwine the two in a "total compensation package," employees divide them into separate issues.

A service premium is not a new idea. For years many organizations have been adding money to base rates to reward long service, but they fail to recognize it as such. The top part of most rate ranges is for service, although few managers or consultants care to admit it. Most of a person's movement through a rate range reflects his or her mastery of job content, but the top portion of the rate range in both automatic and merit progression systems is often simply for long service in that particular job.

The problem can be easily corrected by relabeling these rate ranges and rewording communication to employees. If the top portion of a rate range is indeed designed to recognize the years spent in a particular job, tell employees so. It is more honest and will be more appreciated. Organizations that have rate ranges with no fluff and that pay solely for job content, can easily add a service premium to the top.

Most organizations respect and value long service. That is why we have service awards or benefit increases at benchmark years. But increased benefits reward long service only once a year, at vacation; once every few years, when life insurance increases; or once a career, at retirement. When an organization recognizes the value of long service with a service premium, the individual receives reinforcement with every paycheck.

The psychology of demonstrating the value of long service is far more important than the money, and a service premium doesn't cost all that much. It should be enough to have a psychological impact on long-service employees, but not enough to alienate short-service employees. An approximation is 1 percent for every three years of service. This is more than a gratuity but less than a bribe, and for a small cost we can effect a large shift in attitudes about the fairness of pay.

Nearly every experienced manager or supervisor has at one time tried to appease a long-service employee who has learned that a recent hire or a person with shorter service is earning the same rate. The reply always focuses on benefits—"You get more vacation, first pick of vacation days around the holidays, additional life insurance, a ten-year service pin with a sapphire chip in it . . .." But many long-service employees want special financial consideration for devoting so much of their lives to the organization.

While the concept of a service premium is not especially popular among managers, research shows that most nonmanagers think it is a pretty good idea. The idea is especially popular among blue collar employees who expect to perform the same or similar jobs for the rest of their lives. Chances are if such employees receive service premiums, they will not be tempted to switch organizations simply for a pay increase. (A checklist to help you see how your pay system is working is in Appendix E.)

A Generic Model for Pay Systems Design

A recent analysis confirmed earlier research: The simpler and more straightforward the pay system, the more favorable the attitudes.

Responses to the survey item, "I am paid fairly for the kind of work I do" (Agree, Disagree, ?) are significantly more favorable under these conditions:

- Five or fewer pay grades covering all production and manufacturing employees
- Equal percentage differences among the top rates for all grades (smooth top rate to top rate progression)
- Little or no overlap of grades (top of a grade to the bottom of the next)
- Rapid progression through a range (one year or less).

When companies were in line with the market, then external equity was a nonissue. Internal equity—how the organization's system is designed—is the overriding factor in perceived equity.

Therefore, if you have a complex, erratic and confusing pay system, you need to "de-complex" immediately, if not sooner.

How to Decomplex a Pay System

To improve Attitude Survey results on the item, "I am paid fairly for the kind of work I do," we recommend the following process:

1.   Compare your top rate for the highest pay grade to your community survey market price. If you are equal to or greater than the local norm for the highest paid jobs, then you are safe at the top. Next, compare the top rate for the lowest pay grade and compare it to the community equivalent, and if it matches then you are safe on that end of the distribution. Next, pick the pay grade with the most employees (unless it is one of the two preceding) and compare it to the relevant community data and see if it is satisfactory. If all of the above checks out, then external equity should be a nonissue. If it does not check out, then be prepared to

make needed adjustments during the redesign process. You should be at or 5 percent ahead of the arithmetic mean of the external benchmarks (no higher or lower over a year's period).

2. Form a Project Team composed of managers, supervisors, and employees. We suggest a 10 percent sprinkling of people from all pay grades. If you have relatively few people, this will be one team not to exceed two dozen. If you are larger, form more than one Project Team.

3. Explain to the team that (A) the current pay system design is holding down attitudes, (B) the system will be totally redesigned by the team(s), (C) the team charter is strictly limited to the internal equity issues and they are not to get into external market issues, (D) no other subjects or individual complaints are to be discussed, (E) absolute 100 percent full agreement among everyone on the team or teams is mandatory, and (F) they are to stay at the project until a new design is completed.

4. Explain to the team(s) the results of the research contained in this report. Challenge the team members to create the most simple, straightforward, easy-to-understand pay system they can possibly achieve, with the understanding that the attitudes of the people getting the pay are the foremost concern. Perceived equity is the goal. Forget past practices, excuses and problems, and disregard everything management or the human resources people have said, including job descriptions, job titles, job evaluation methodology and any references to what other companies or divisions have been doing.

5. The team discusses what each person actually is doing in his or her work. Reach agreement and understanding on the essential similarities and essential differences of the various jobs. The team is not to proceed any further until this step is complete. Group the jobs that are essentially similar in content and context (similar functions and skills) and give each cluster a positive title or name.

6. The next step is rank ordering the jobs, but to accomplish this requires a criterion or criteria upon which to rank. The team must discuss and reach consensus and understanding on the single criterion that is the key element. This will be used for the initial and primary ranking. If there is a second criterion, it will be used to fine tune the basic rank order. The usual criterion is the time it takes to learn to perform the job to its fullest. The other criteria will vary from safety to physical effort to prior knowledge and skills. However, it is up to the team to determine these.

7. Ranking against the criterion is the next step. Each team member must have an input, and the discussion of the proper rank order will be hot and heavy. Leaders must avoid letting one or two verbal or aggressive types force their department's job too high in the combined ranking. The objective is to get a combined ranking of all the jobs in all the departments. Do not let the team go back to any prior step or move beyond this step until there is consensus.

8. If there are several Project Teams, they may or may not get the same combined ranking. To get consensus among all the teams, take a few

members of each team and put them together to work out any differences in the ranking. When this is achieved, go back to the separate teams and make any adjustments necessary and apply the other criteria, if any, to make the final adjustments.

9. Have each team now group the ranked jobs into pay grades. This should be arbitrarily limited to five maximum and fewer if possible. The goal is the least number of pay grades that is reasonable and workable. Loop the results through all the teams if there is more than one. Get consensus.

10. Apply the minimum and top pay rates to each pay grade, according to the market price survey. If you are way off base to the low side, you may want to catch up over a two-year period. Keep the spread from the bottom to the top of the range short at the lowest pay grade and longer at the top pay grade. It should approximate the learning curve that was used to rank the jobs.

11. Help the teams prepare a simple presentation for all the other employees. The communication of the new system should be done by first line supervisors with the assistance of the other employees who were involved on the teams. The presentations to the various work groups should all be made at the same time. The presenters should give a "blow by blow" description of what was done, how it was done, all the discussions and logic involved in the project and why it came out the way it did. The movement of individuals to the new system then takes place, and the base hourly rates change as necessary. Red circle those over the new pay grade and move up those who fall below.

12. Refer all questions or complaints to a team member, since it is their project and their product.

13. Hold a party for all the project team members. For help with the ingredients of your pay system, see Appendix F.

Benefits and Incentives

In the typical unionized corporation, different employee groups receive different benefit packages. It is a more common practice in unionfree companies to provide the same benefit programs for all employees, regardless of their status in the organization, from the highest-paid to the lowest-paid employee. This avoids an unnecessary delineation of class distinctions that enhances the management-labor dichotomy. Furthermore, it is the lower-paid people who can least afford an illness in the family, or a temporary loss of income due to injury or illness. People in lower job classifications have a greater need for effective benefit programs than do executives, who are often in a financial position to take care of economic disasters resulting from illness. For many years, the concept of paternalism has been rejected as archaic, yet the people who need such things as life and hospitalization insurance are least likely to be able to afford them. Although it may be paternalistic in a sense, therefore, it is necessary to provide these things to employees as part of the total compensation package in order to have an effective program. It takes very few instances of serious illness or injury involving an employee or family member to offset many good management practices. Even though there are a number of federal government programs as well as state plans for the protection of low-income people during periods of illness or injury, most of these operate at a relatively low level of protection. Possibly, in the future, adequate pension programs and health plans will be provided by governmental programs, but until that time comes, employers will do well to voluntarily provide benefit protection for people who are potential union members. Once again, the costs can be offset through techniques for improving productivity.

Only "basic" benefits (medical, life and disability insurance; paid time off; retirement) are needed to stay unionfree. Fringe benefits (recreation, service awards, Christmas parties) do little except direct money away from a competitive basic compensation package.

Incentive systems of various kinds have been tried by management to encourage higher productivity. In many cases, the removal of an individual incentive piece-rate system has resulted in higher productivity than the incentive scheme was able to produce. One reason for this is the assumption behind incentive schemes that most people do not produce at more than 60 percent of their capability. When one makes this kind of assumption about human beings, the facts tend to produce exactly the results that the assumption stated. There is, however, a value in terms of productivity and the maintenance of unionfree status in *group* incentive schemes, such as profit sharing. While there are many forms of profit sharing, most of them return to the employees an additional form of economic reward on the basis of their contribution to the overall profits of the organization. When there is a relatively stable workforce and a simple product technology involved, these plans can be established on a small-group basis. But in today's integrated organizations, with complex technologies and changing workforces, company-wide profit-sharing schemes hold more promise.

Gainsharing and profit-sharing schemes should be kept simple. The money should be protected, and the individual should have an opportunity to spend some of it and not have to put all of it in a retirement fund. The accounting and the arithmetic involved should be simple and intelligible to the people who are receiving the benefits, not just to the designer and to management. Very few unionized organizations have profit-sharing plans, and, if properly communicated, the benefits of a profit-sharing plan can be a powerful deterrent to the introduction of unionization into the company.

A Systems Approach to Gainsharing

Quick-fix prescriptions for human resource problems are so common that we sometimes seem to have management by best seller. Just buy a copy of the newest book, read the instructions, pull the little red string, apply to the problem, and wait for things to get better. But just like Band-Aids, they do not fix the problem; rather they cover it up while nature provides the cure. Band-Aids are useful so long as one remembers their proper function. So it seems to be with gainsharing and other nontraditional approaches to compensation. Many managers rush to apply gainsharing in their organizations, and then wait for the magic cure.

What are we trying to accomplish?

What precisely are the human resource problems that gainsharing is supposed to fix? What is the origin of gainsharing? Why is it now so popular among American managers? What other options should an organization consider when confronted by significant human productivity and quality challenges? Is gainsharing simply another Band-Aid to cover up mediocrity, or will it truly improve organizational effectiveness? Managers should ask themselves these tough questions when evaluating the need for and appropriateness of gainsharing for their organizations.

At CVR, we have defined three levels of strategic thinking. At the top of the strategic hierarchy are the organization's objectives. Objectives are closely tied to the organization's mission or vision, and represent the givens. Next come the strategies, which define what has to be done in order to achieve the objectives. Finally, we have the tactics, which describe how the strategies will be achieved. Tactics are the tools and techniques that are used to implement strategy. At what level of strategic thinking does gainsharing belong? Our conclusion is that gainsharing belongs at the tactical level. Our experience and research indicates that gainsharing is one of many tools that may be appropriate for the implementation of identified business strategies. This perspective is important in order to ensure organizational clarity about gainsharing.

The systems view looks at phenomena in terms of relationships and integration, rather than as isolated entities. This is a process perspective. Gainsharing does not exist in a vacuum. Managers who introduce gainsharing should take the time first to understand the dynamic cultural interactions and interrelationships that organizations exhibit. It would be a serious mistake for managers to view gainsharing in a purely mechanistic fashion. Managers who assume that gainsharing is analogous to Newton's clockwork model of the universe (you simply wind it up and it ticks along indefinitely on its own merry way) may be introducing a lot more discontinuity into their organizations than they bargained for. Gainsharing is not just a mechanical or mathematically elegant solution to human resource problems. Gainsharing exists in human perception and organizational dynamics, not in a realm of mathematical certainty. Numbers are integral to Gainsharing design, but the numbers merely represent reality; they are not themselves reality. Our search of the literature reveals several surveys that dealt with *managers'* views about gainsharing. To our knowledge, we are the first to conduct research on the perceptions of the *employees* who work in organizations that have introduced gainsharing.

The Reality of Gainsharing: Are the Claims Real?

There are few definitive research results to support the "gain" part of gainsharing. There are true or accurate reports of gains in the order of 20 to 25 percent improvement in productivity; however, these claims of success often ignore the time frame for the improvements. When one digs deeply into the limited data available, one often finds that the 20 or 25 percent improvement is over a five-year or longer period; This translates to a 4 or 5 percent gain per year—certainly not highly dramatic or significant.

Assuming there are organizations that did get significant performance improvements after implementing gainsharing, how long will these improvements last? There is anecdotal evidence that gainsharing runs out of steam in about three years. What then? The author has uncovered one organization that applied gainsharing as part of a last-ditch effort to stay in business. For the first two years of gainsharing, nothing improved. Then the plant manager was replaced with a strong people-oriented individual. Almost overnight, efficiency gains were realized, and the gainsharing plan began paying substantial bonuses. Obviously, gainsharing in this instance was the dependent variable in the equation of organizational dynamics, and not the spark plug that energized a process of continual improvement.

In 1981, the General Accounting Office of the federal government published its study of various gainsharing plans. It concluded that gainsharing is not a substitute either for sound or progressive management or for competitive wages and benefits.

For many organizations, the introduction of gainsharing may represent a significant discontinuity relative to these traditional issues:

- Managerial roles (much more delegation and decentralization)
- Information sharing ("want to know," not "need to know")
- Employee communication (disclosing the financial bottom line)
- Goal setting and goal sharing (mutual participation)
- Closing the loops on expectations (performance feedback)
- Delegation of responsibility for quality (fewer inspectors)
- A climate of mutual trust (reduce "we versus they" mentality)

Criteria for Successful Approaches

The criteria for success begins with eliminating any negatives in employee relations that may exist, before accentuating the positives. This means positive morale, competent management, a carefully selected and well-trained workforce, clear performance expectations, solid supervision, good base pay and benefits, and the removal of any "we versus they" thinking so as to have high levels of trust. Then, and only then, should the additional gainsharing be entertained. In other words, gainsharing should not be considered in mediocre organizations, but it might be appropriate for good ones that are already on the

Making Unions Unnecessary

path toward excellence. Truly excellent organizations may be beyond gainsharing and ready for true Profit Sharing (see Figure 2).

Characteristics of Gainsharing Plans

Effective gainsharing plans have the following characteristics:

- Include all employees in the plan
- Give everyone an equal bonus (same percentage)
- Create a clear connection of performance to reward
- Pay the bonuses on a timely basis (monthly/quarterly)
- Make the criteria fair and relevant to the business
- Make the criteria easy to understand (simplicity)
- Make the criteria relevant to economic reality
- Maximize employee involvement opportunities
- Share information widely (almost to excess)
- Provide extensive training to make gains feasible

Figure 2

Pay Systems

LEVELS OF ORGANIZATIONAL DEVELOPMENT

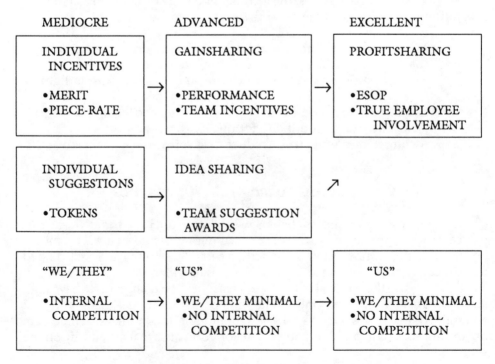

- Make the connection in the mind of each employee between his or her work and bonus
- Design company's plan for its own uniqueness
- Adapt company's communications to employee value systems
- Measure employee attitudes before and after

Summary and Key Points

Benefits are often the subject of union negotiations and organizing drives. Money is important to everyone, although it is important for various reasons, according to the individual's values. The key factors related to pay and benefits are the predetermination of the levels of compensation to be attained and the public statement of goals that the company commits itself to achieve. Voluntarily making improvements in wages and benefits on a regularly scheduled basis is a powerful factor in the maintenance of unionfree status. It avoids the necessity of people taking collective action to place pressure on management to make improvements.

Whether pay should be based on performance or service depends on whether the individual can make an impact on the performance of her or his job. When the individual's attributes, motivation, and attitudes have relatively little impact on performance levels, the service progression or single-rate approaches to pay are most consistent with equitable compensation and the maintenance of unionfree status. On the other hand, when the individual has a significant degree of freedom to do well or to do marginally in the productive performance of his job, merit pay does hold some incentive value. Merit pay absolutely requires that individual performance be measurable in a way the employee and supervisor both understand and perceive as equitable.

Performance for pay appears to be the system that employees are most likely to perceive as equitable. Because job standards are precise, and because personnel are carefully and properly selected and placed, many of the problems inherent in merit pay and automatic progression are eliminated.

Proper pay and benefit levels are necessary for the maintenance of unionfree status. In and of themselves, however, these two key factors will not suffice to keep employees from collective activity. Your pay and benefits Self-Audit 8 is in Appendix A.

CHAPTER 12

EQUAL EMPLOYMENT OPPORTUNITY

The concept of equal employment opportunity is broader than Title VII of the Civil Rights Act. It is also an area in which people often turn to unions for help. When they feel that they are being discriminated against, concerted activity on the part of protected classes of employees, such as women and minorities, may take the form of collective action to join a union or the form of complaint to the Equal Employment Opportunity Commission. In other words, discrimination in employment conditions against any group may lead to unionization efforts, class-action suits, or to both at the same time.

Achieving the goal of maintaining unionfree status, therefore, requires attention to the areas of discrimination and advancement opportunities. Union organizing patterns may take the form of appealing to the disadvantaged group, particularly when a majority of the employees are within one of the protected classes. For example, it is conceivable that female employees could take the route of unionization to achieve their ends rather than appealing to the federal law covering discrimination in employment.

Perhaps a more effective means of viewing equal employment opportunity is to define it more broadly than Title VII of the Civil Rights Act or the National Labor Relations Act. The concept of equality in employment opportunity must be extended to all individuals as well as groups. Inequality in the treatment of employees based on differences between salaried and hourly employees, management and labor, or any other traditional, however artificial, distinctions between individuals, and the tendency to classify people according to stereotyped patterns, creates gaps and disparities. Differences in pay practices, benefit programs, communications, advancement opportunities, and the content of work are all forms of unequal treatment. Many of these are such traditional and longstanding practices that are not perceived by management, but an increasing number of people are becoming aware of disparities in treatment.

As shifts in value systems occur among the population, away from the more traditional, circumscribed views of the world to the more enlightened viewpoint of humanity and the individual, the concept of equal employment opportunities will be broadened to comprehend many other conditions of employment. Just as laws regulating management-labor relationships were enacted years ago, the treatment of men and women, black and white, old and young, educated and unskilled is now subject to a federal legalistic approach.

The majority of these laws came into being because of the slowness of management to change and the unresponsiveness of people to other people. To avoid additional legislation the only appropriate answer is a more rapid rate of progress on the part of the corporations. Attempts to delay progress or to evade or stall the law are likely to result in further legal pressure on corporations to make their judgments about people on the basis of performance rather than on arbitrary criteria.

Summary and Key Points

Equal employment opportunity is covered by Title VII of the Civil Rights Act and the National Labor Relations Act. Both are means to the same end: Equality of opportunity based on the ability of the individual to make a contribution to the organization, rather than on an irrelevant factor that does not affect job performance. It is possible for an organization to have both Title VII and unionization activities going on at the same time, both of them pursuing the objective of enforcing the right of people to be judged for what they do rather than who they are. Shifts in value systems and in the views that people have of one another and their relationship to society and the corporation will accelerate these trends and increase the need for management to make rapid progress in this area.

CHAPTER 13

FACILITIES AND JOB SECURITY

Traditionally, management has treated itself better in terms of facilities, working conditions, and job security than it has the people being managed. Managers have worked in comfortable, well-decorated offices while people in other job classifications were working in facilities that not only lacked esthetic appeal but often made little or no provision for environmental climate control and even safety. In response to management's neglect in this area, the Occupational Safety and Health Act was enacted, adding an additional set of regulations that management must cope with.

Companies are beginning to realize that drawing distinctions between individuals and emphasizing these distinctions by providing various status symbols reinforce the management-labor dichotomy. Many unionfree organizations have adopted the policy of combining office and factory operations, having single dining facilities, common parking facilities, common entrances, and much open space and glass partitioning so that management and other employees may see and mingle with one another in an effort to reduce status differences. Of course, there are in fact differences in status and pay between management and labor, but it is unnecessary and counterproductive to reinforce these differences through the excessive use of status symbols.

If one of the main means of maintaining unionfree status is the integration of all the employees of the organization so that they feel as much a part of the company as top management, removing physical barriers and disparity in treatment and working conditions are important strategic approaches to the goal.

Job Security

Employee concerns about the future of the company or their future within the company come in two delicious flavors: fear of being involuntarily terminated (fired), and concern about being caught in a layoff or plant/office closing.

Concerns over being fired are an excellent motivational tool—for problem employees. For the other 95 percent, it is ridiculous to practice management-by-fear to encourage employees to pursue the goals of the organization—or else! Fear of arbitrary action can and should keep marginal performers on their toes, but it can also keep good performers (or potentially excellent performers) on their heels. When good employees witness bodies falling all around them on a regular basis, the natural (and intelligent) reaction is to assume a low profile until such time as decent employment can be found. It is the lack of a systematic approach to due process in corrective actions that causes most of the employee nervousness. Due process includes a clearly stated set of ground rules—behavioral expectations—communicated to all employees, coupled with a corrective action program that sets forth a step-by-step method for dealing fairly with infractions. If any of these ingredients is missing, so too will feelings of job security.

Even when employees do not fear being individually singled out for placement into the ranks of the unemployed, equal negative impact can result when they believe that the organization, or their positions in it, might not be around next week. Layoffs for any reason are sure to cause job security concerns, even though most people do understand that business cycles are often unavoidable. Cutbacks or facilities closing at other locations are an integral part of this concern. The maximum level of unfavorable attitude response, which will likely last over a long period of time, comes from layoff situation procedures that are subjective, arbitrary or constantly changing. Layoffs based solely on management perception of individual performance can and will make even high performers nervous.

Recurring cycles of reorganization, acquisition and divestitures are also regularly cited as habits not conducive to strong job security feelings among employees. This seems to have the greatest effect on middle and upper managers and staff employees because this group is most likely to become redundant when someone at the top starts changing signals. This is particularly true when there is a history of a periodic cycle of new "clean-sweep" managers bringing in their own personal philosophies (e.g., "Who needs a human resources staff?") or personal friends to bump out unknown incumbents. In this environment, or any other kind for that matter, maximum uneasiness comes from employee perceptions that the primary decision makers are gifted with above-average incompetence. The belief that guesswork, trial and error, and change for change's sake are the prevailing management methodology is not likely to inspire employees to mentally or physically lock in for the long term.

One job security issue of more recent vintage that is being more frequently identified by employees is taking just-in-time (JIT) delivery systems to extremes. While JIT is an excellent concept that has served many Japanese and U.S. companies well, improperly used it can and has created havoc with employee attitudes and production/shipping schedules. Tight JIT scheduling into and through the operation, with no contingency plan except shut-downs on an unpredictable basis because of supplier failures, is rapidly creeping into many organizations and just as rapidly causing employee unrest.

Summary and Key Points

Eliminating useless physical barriers and "we versus they" symbols helps create an "us" environment. It should also improve communications, for if "out of sight is out of mind," then increased visibility should lead to familiarity, and perhaps to trust.

CHAPTER 14

MAKING UNIONS UNNECESSARY

In short, then, unions are necessary only when we make them necessary. And remaining unionfree doesn't require giving away the company store, because nothing we have been discussing is very costly. It isn't necessary to have higher benefits than anybody else to keep the union out; it isn't necessary to overpay. The means of improving communications that we've discussed are not costly. The open door is cheap. The job posting system is inexpensive. Underwriting training and education does not cost much. Letting people participate in systems design provides excellent returns on the time invested.

We aren't buying anybody off, and we certainly aren't threatening them. We're just saying, "Let's close this gap between management and labor. Let's see what we can do to meet people's needs without conflicting with the goals of the organization." And if we play it straight and run it clean, we'll be making it unnecessary for employees to look to a union for the things they aren't getting from management.

In short, we can *make unions unnecessary.*

III

APPENDIXES

APPENDIX A

SELF-AUDITS

1. Why Be Unionfree?

Do I really know why the company should be unionfree?
What do the other managers think about being unionfree?
What has been my personal experience with unions?
If we have had prior union organizing attempts, what were the reasons? What have we done to eliminate these reasons?
What are the attitudes of our employees about unions? How do we know?
What effects would unionization have on our productivity?
What is the reputation of our organization in the community? In the industry? With those who work here?
What is the reputation of our organization with our customers? With our competitors?
Has the subject of remaining unionfree been discussed among management? If not, why not? If so, what action items came out of the discussion?
Is there a tendency in our organization to blame the union for any past union problems? Where does the blame really belong?
Are the federal government and laws blamed for employee relations problems? If so, what should we do to refocus our thinking?
Have we been teaching our people to be unionfree or unionprone?
Who in our community/industry is unionfree? Unionized? Are they considered "excellent"?
Is our management committed to "dealing with people directly, not through third parties"? How do we know for sure? Do we know who is committed and who is not? Do we know why some are not committed?
What is the percentage of unionized employees in our community/industry/state?
What special problems/advantages does this present for our organization?
What type of coordination do we have or should we have with other organizations in our community?
If we are located in a highly unionized area, do we intend to confer with the union organizations to explain our propeople, unionfree posture? If not, why not?
Do our managers/supervisors know the history of employee relations in America and our own organization's history with unions?

Making Unions Unnecessary

If there is relatively little unionization in our area, what are the advantages of a joint venture seminar or conference with other local unionfree organizations to coordinate all unionfree efforts? Have we further developed the idea and presented it to other companies?
If we are considering moving or expanding a union operation, are we considering a site selection with the unionfree objective in mind?
If we are moving or expanding, have we designed our human resources policies and programs to be unionfree, or are we simply relocating management attitudes and policies that emulate the old union style?
Have all managers/supervisors been taught the basics of labor law? If not, why not? If so, how much do they remember? Is it time for a refresher?

2. Goal: No Unions

Does my organization have a clearly stated goal of being unionfree? If not, why not?
If there is no goal or philosophy, how should it be written for our type of organization and employee population?
If there is a goal statement or policy about remaining unionfree, what does it say?
If there is no written goal in the Management by Objectives System, why isn't there?
Has our written goal been communicated and understood at all levels of the organization—Corporate? Division? Plant/Branch? If not, why not?
How have we ensured that we have complete commitment to remain unionfree from all managers and supervisors?
If there is no clear commitment, what will it take to ensure it?
Who will have to be involved in gaining commitment? When can we accomplish that?
How do we communicate our philosophy or goal to employees? Is it seen as an actual goal or a "lip service" goal? How do we know?
How do we reaffirm our commitment throughout the year? If we don't reaffirm our commitment, how should we?
How do we help reluctant supervisors and managers to buy into our unionfree goal?
What do we do if they don't buy in? What *should* we do if they don't buy in?
How can we test supervisors/managers for this kind of commitment during preemployment interviews?
How do we cope with nearby unionized organizations or the community mentality?
Are there any special problems with headquarters that have to be overcome? Are we working to overcome them?
Each manager should ponder this: What is my own personal position about management/labor thinking? Am I geared to be unionfree or unionprone? If

we do not have a clearly communicated policy/philosophy, when and how are we going to get one, and what part should I play in it?
How have we communicated to everyone—Meetings? Handbook? Supervisory meetings? Community newspapers? New employee orientation?
What style and content should our statement have?
Are there any special situations we need to be aware of?
Have we discussed "authorization cards" with everyone? If not, why not?
Have people been informed of their right to sign or not sign? If so, in what ways? If not, why not?
In our communications about preferring to be unionfree, are we being "antiunion" or straightforwardly, positively "unionfree"? How do our people see it? How do we know for sure?

3. The Road from We/They to Us

Do we have a Management vs. Labor mentality? If so, where did it originate?
What will have to be done to change it to an "us" mentality?
Are we using accounting terminology such as "direct labor," "workers" and "hourly," or military terminology such as "troops," "chain of command," "leave of absence," "divisions?" Are we aware of the connotations they carry and the affect they may have on our attitudes and behavior?
What do we have to do to change these words and the negative assumptions behind them?
What steps must we take to eradicate the "we vs. they" gap?
Do our memoranda, handbooks, daily language, etc., reflect the "we/they" 1930s way of thinking? How can we change this?
What do we mean by "employees"—who are we thinking of? Do we include management? If not, why not?
Are there any managers/supervisors who may have to be confronted about their attitudes regarding people?
Who are they, by name? Who will confront them, and when? Are we prepared to deal stringently with those who will not change their negative attitudes?
Do we have any special problems with any parts of the company that are currently unionized? What kinds of problems are they, and what can we do to resolve them quickly and positively?
Are we teaching people to "think union," or have we analyzed our programs to see if the unionfree concept is built into everything we do?
Is the relationship with people at all organizational levels based on trust or exploitation? If the relationship is built on exploitation, how can we change it to one of trust?
Are people considered "resources to be used in production," or are they treated with respect and dignity?
When we design or evaluate our programs, is it for the "big wheels" or for all the other employees?
Do we "already have all the answers"? Or are we concerned with asking the

"right questions"? Who should we be asking?
Are we prepared to change now what needs changing? If not, how can we become prepared?
What is the "why" behind each of our policies? What are the implicit and explicit assumptions? If they are negative or neutral, how can we add a positive influence?
What would happen if negative policies were eliminated? Why not eliminate them?
Do our supervisors use the policies written by our managers, or do they only pay them lip service and work around them? If many of our supervisors work around our policies, how can the policies be changed to make them more useful and positive to those who work with them?
Which policies cause the most friction among our people? Why do they cause friction? What should be done to eliminate the friction?
How many of our negative policies have become self-fulfilling prophecies?
What attitudes and behaviors would we like employees to have? How can we turn positive policies into self-fulfilling prophecies?

4. Employee Communications

Open Door

Do we have an open door system? If so, how many doors are really open? If not, why not?
Do we permit direct access to upper management? If not, why not?
Have we communicated our open door or other problem resolution policy to employees? If so, in what form—handbook, orientation, department meeting? If not, why not?
Do we support supervisors and managers when a correct decision has been made? Do we reverse incorrect decisions? Do our supervisors trust that we will be fair? How do we know? Do our employees trust that we won't arbitrarily side with the supervisor? Again, how do we know?
How many open door cases have gone beyond the immediate supervisor to Human Resources and/or upper management? Do we feel this number is excessive? How many should we expect?
Do we have any particular departments, supervisors, divisions, etc., that seem to run unusually high or low complaint rates? Are there clusters of problems? If so, what are their causes and general nature? Are they recurring? What are we doing to correct the situation?
Do our people believe our open door system is sincere? Do they have faith in our integrity? Have we asked them, to be certain?
Does our management truly support the open door system or do they only pay it lip service? What evidence do we have?
Have we successfully avoided employee grievance committees?
Do we know who our chronic complainers are and why they complain? Are their

complaints justified, indicating we may have policy problems, or are they merely wasting valuable time and energy?

Supervisors' Skills

Do our supervisors have good interpersonal skills? How do we know? If they don't, what is being done about it? What *should* be done about it?

Do our supervisors have the necessary interpersonal skills and confidence to serve as the key information exchange for their workgroups? If not, what can we do to help them develop both skills and confidence?

Do our first line supervisors have credibility among their workgroups as a trusted source of information?

Is communication within a workgroup upward, downward and lateral? How do we know? If it isn't, what needs to be done to ensure it?

Meetings

Are supervisors required to hold daily/weekly/monthly meetings? What should be the nature of the meetings? Have we asked employees what information they want and need?

Do we hold cross-departmental meetings to acquaint people with other individuals and operations?

Are unit meetings held regularly? If not, why not? What is the best schedule—monthly or quarterly?

What prepared materials are furnished to department and unit managers to aid them in conducting the meetings? What materials are needed? How do we know?

Does top management occasionally participate in the meetings to improve the visibility of higher level management and/or headquarters people? If not, how can we get them to do this?

How are communications among the various shifts? Are there strategic advantages to overlapping meetings among shifts? Have we tried it to see? Have we asked the people and supervisors on different shifts to see what they think?

Employee Handbook

Do we have a handbook? Where did it come from? Who wrote it? What assumptions about people are implied throughout it? Have any of them become self-fulfilling prophecies?

Is it readable for most people? Is the writing style too complex? How do we know for sure?

Is the book too long? Do benefit program descriptions clutter up the basic policies and procedures? Do our people read it? Again, how do we know?

Making Unions Unnecessary

Who participated in the development of the handbook? Were employees of all levels in on the development and editing? If not, why not?
Was the book tested on nonsupervisory people to see if the content and style were compatible with their needs, interests and values?
What steps should be taken to find out if the current book is of any value to people in the organization?
Do the policies described in the handbook fit actual daily practices? How do we know? If not, what policy changes should be made?
Is the book used in new-employee orientation? Is it used or referred to in department meetings to further explain the "whys" of organizational practices?

Ad Hoc Committees

Have we tried ad hoc communications committees? If so, did they serve any productive, useful purpose? How can we make them more effective and useful? If not, when can we try one?
Do we have committees that are learning to "bargain"? What are we doing to stop this development?
If we have committees that are getting "out of control," what is our strategy for correcting the situation?
What are the benefits of the ad hoc committee approach? How can we best use ad hoc committees? When can we start?
Are the committees removing or creating a "we vs. they" dichotomy? How can we be sure? Have we asked our people what they think about it?

Other

Do we use video as an integral part of our communications system? If not, why not, and when can we try it?
Have we considered doing a jobholders' report and holding a jobholders' meeting? What effect would they have on our people? Why don't we try it?

5. Performance Standards

Are we really able to "objectively" measure performance differences? "Objective" according to whom—the rater or the person being rated?
What performance standards and appraisal system/form are we using? Where did it come from? Is it working? How do we know?
Were our supervisors and their workgroups involved in determining the current performance standards and measurements? If not, why not?
Do our supervisors and nonmanagement employees feel that our current performance standards and measurements systems are fair? How do we know?
Could our supervisors and their workgroups determine several different

measurement systems specific to each job? Have we tried to? If not, why not? Is our performance appraisal form generalized to cover so many different kinds of work that it really measures nothing?

Are we still trying to measure such questionable concepts as attitude, dependability, initiative, etc., that are nearly impossible to assess accurately?

Does our appraisal form use words to describe degrees of goodness/badness such as "commendable," "superior," "average," "meets requirements," "competent," etc., that may communicate one thing to the rater and another to the person being rated?

Can we clearly define and measure speed and accuracy for each different job? Have we tried? If not, why not?

Will our current system for setting and measuring standards hold up in court? How do we know?

Have we initiated a process for defining and measuring performance excellence? Do we expect performance excellence? If not, why not? If so, have we clearly communicated this to our people? Have we set examples?

Do we have a binary rating system with clearly defined "required performance" and "unacceptable performance"? If not, why not? Do we know what is required and unacceptable for each individual job? If not, why not, and when are we going to find out?

If our standards are inappropriate, what has to be done to get them changed? Who should start the process—management or a third party? How long can we afford to wait?

Are we arbitrarily forcing a bell-shaped normal distribution curve? Do we tell supervisors and managers that only a certain number of people can be rated high? If so, why do we do this? What effect does it have on various workgroups? How do supervisors view this practice? Have we asked them?

Does our current system enforce mediocrity or encourage excellence? Does our productivity support our answer? Why are we willing to accept less than top performance from anyone?

If we use a five- or ten-point rating scale, can we see how it has become a self-fulfilling prophecy? How many of our people were rated five or ten? What does that tell us?

Have we witnessed negative changes in behavior by employees seeking psychological equity? Have we ever done it ourselves? How do we expect supervisors and managers to deal with such situations? How can our performance standards and appraisal system be redesigned to eliminate this syndrome?

How often are our employees appraised? How often do they feel they should be appraised? Have we asked them?

Is performance excellence a qualitative goal in our organization? If not, why not? If so, do our people know it? Does management support it? Do our employee relations systems support it? Does top management serve as an example? Do we reward those who achieve performance excellence?

6. Consistency in Work Rules Administration

To what extent do we have "inconsistency"? How do we know?
How many days or percentage of scheduled hours allowed off before corrective, progressive "discipline" is taken? How did we arrive at this number? Do our people feel it is fair?
What is the average absenteeism/tardiness in each department? What is our goal? How far is each department from the goal? Why are some so far off the goal, and how can they bring absenteeism down?
What patterns are developing—by shift/supervisor/unit? Are they positive or negative? What are we doing about negative patterns?
What has been communicated to people about attendance? Is our policy in the handbook? Do our people understand it? Do our supervisors follow the policy? If not, why not?
Do we follow the same guidelines in the office as in the plant? If not, why not?
Have we given supervisors policies and procedures that can be administered easily and consistently? Have they helped design these policies and procedures? If not, why not?
What behaviors do we consider "correctable"? Why do we feel they are correctable?
Are they in writing? Are they clearly written to avoid misinterpretation? Is the list too long?
Have we reached agreement among management/supervision as to what is correctable behavior and what is not?
Do we handle minor correctable disruptions of productivity and "acts offensive to other employees" by due process or by termination? How do our employees feel we should handle it?
Can we use the "no-fault" attendance approach to achieve consistency rather than a case-by-case or "excused/unexcused" method? If not, why not?
If we use an "excused/unexcused" method, do we know what we consider an unexcused absence? Do employees know? Are we consistent? How do supervisors feel about it? Why don't we change it?
Does the nature of our organization require any special kinds of work rules? If so, why, and what are they? Are the assumptions behind them positive or negative?
Have we been consistent in past practices and precedents?

7. Growth Opportunity and Advancement

So What Are You Gonna Do?

Is promotion as integral a part of our pay system as it should be? If not, what can we do to integrate it better?
Are we overselling upward mobility and "getting ahead in the world" to people who would be more effective and better satisfied to stay where they are?

What is our promotion policy? Do we really have one? Is it consistent? Do our people understand and respect it? How do we know?

What do our people feel is the basis of our promotion system—qualifications, favoritism or seniority? Have we asked them?

Have we asked our people if they think our promotion system is fair? If not, why not?

Do we have clear, precise performance standards and measurements that allow us to base promotions on qualifications? If not, why not? Does a lack of clear, precise standards cause us to rely on the union-prone seniority system or inconsistent appointment-type promotions?

Do we use a posting and bidding system? If not, why not? If so, is it used consistently and with integrity? Do our people think so?

Do our posted descriptions give sufficient details on required skills, education, experience, pay range, etc., to aid employees in making a decision to bid?

Do our rules on bidding intimidate employees and keep them from attempting to bid? How do we know?

Do our people feel there are opportunities for those who want to get ahead? Again, how do we know?

Do we offer career development and planning for interested employees? Are employees aware of it? Do they know where to go for help?

Do we recognize supervisors for developing and promoting people in their workgroups? If not, why not?

Do we hire from the outside only when promotion from within is inappropriate?

Do we have a system to identify all potential candidates within our organization for a promotional opportunity? If not, who should develop it, and how soon can it be done?

Do we hire employees whose ambitions match the realistic promotional opportunities?

Have we validated testing procedures for our various jobs? If not, why not?

Does our promotion system pose EEO or other legal risks? How do we know? Have all our managers and supervisors been informed of the relevant laws?

Do we use a trial period for promotions? If not, why not? If so, how many prospects failed the trial period? Were they happy to be able to return to their former jobs?

Do we provide the training needed to help potentially qualified people become qualified?

When people with promotion aspirations are rejected, are they given honest reasons why and told specifically what they must do to improve?

Are we "honest" with those whom we know we will never promote?

How many demotions have we had in the last five years? Where are these people now? What are their attitudes?

If our employees turn down promotions, are they "punished" in any way, such as being blacklisted from future promotions, denied responsibility for coveted projects, or denied access to necessary information? If so, what can we do to prevent this?

8. Pay and Benefits

Pay:

Which are we really watching—numbers or attitudes?
What are we communicating to employees about our pay system? What should we be communicating?
What are the perceptions of our organization's employees about our pay system? How do we know for sure?
Have we or should we survey people's attitudes and value systems to find out?
Who have we designed our pay system to satisfy and to be understood by—management or the rest of the people?
When we think of the pay system, whose system is it? Whose should it be?
Who prepared our job descriptions—outside or resident "experts"?
Do we have more job descriptions than are necessary? How do we know how many are necessary? How much overlap do we have?
Are we teaching the "not my job" syndrome?
Do we have more job titles than are really necessary? Have we simply copied the unionized approach?
Are we naming people for machines or for the work they do while using machines? Are we giving titles we would be proud to have?
Can we, by these processes, create such a distinctively positive atmosphere that a union climate would have difficulty developing?
What is our approach to job evaluation—are we using a "scientific" system that may be "accurate" but is incomprehensible to most people?
What system are we using now? Points/factors/Hay Guide Chart/National Metal Trades? Do we really understand them? Can we explain them clearly?
What do the rest of our people think? How do we know?
Could we use simple ranking and get better perceived equity? Have we tried it? If not, should we?
Were any of the supervisors involved in the job evaluation process, or was it a "secret" corporate function with committees composed of top management and outside consultants?
Do our outside consultants really know our jobs? How do we know? Do our top managers really know our jobs? How do we know?
How many job grades (pay classes) do we now have? Why do we have that number?
Could we get by with fewer? Are the differences so insignificant that no one knows what we are trying to do?
Would fewer grades and less range overlap get better perception of equity?
Could different grade levels have different progression times to better match learning curves?
What pay survey method are we using? Are we concentrating on local surveys? If not, why not?
Do we have comparability in job content to assure external equity? How do we know?

Have we selected our survey companies appropriately? How do we know whether their jobs are the same as or similar to ours?

Do we or are we willing to communicate the results of the pay survey to all concerned? If not, why not?

Can we explain why some companies pay higher in the community than we do?

Can we answer people's questions about our pay policy?

Can we explain why other communities pay higher rates?

Have we set a pay policy in line with the survey average (arithmetic mean)?

Do we schedule the rate change at the same time each year so that people know when to expect an increase in pay rates? If not, why not?

Have we let everyone know the rate structure? If not, why not? If so, how do we communicate it?

Have we put predictability and intelligibility into our pay system?

Do we have a service premium? If not, have we considered one? What percentage of our employees has more than five, ten and fifteen years of service?

Can we move people through the pay system individually by skill acquisitions (multicraft/multiskill)? If not, why not?

Do we have measurements to objectively determine skill/craft levels?

If we have piece-rates, are they necessary or are they a cop-out for quality supervision? What would happen if we eliminated piece rates? How do our people feel about piece rates?

Have we considered that different methods of making individual pay increases may be necessary for different job families, or have we simply applied one approach when more than one might be more effective?

Would a bonus-type merit system be better than putting the money into the base rate?

Are our standards precise enough so that individual performance can be measured for a bonus system?

Who controls an individual's productivity—the individual, the supervisor or the system? Who do we want to control it?

Does the equipment or job design really contribute more to individual performance than the person? If so, do our employees have the equipment and job designs they need to be effective?

Could we use a version of a group productivity improvement bonus system? Should we?

Would a more frequent bonus system, on top of an automatic progression, have more effect on output per person/group? Have we asked our people what they think about it? Do we recognize that the key to a unionfree pay system is based on maximum feasible simplicity? Does our system show that we do?

Benefits:

What criteria are we using to set benefit policies? Do they follow the local norms or national norms? Which norms better serve the needs of our employees?

Do we have all the basic benefits necessary to remain unionfree? If not, why not, and how soon can we add whatever is missing?

What benefit distinctions now exist among exempt, nonexempt and hourly benefit programs? Are these distinctions really necessary? Are they perpetrating a "we/they" gap and causing negative employee attitudes?

What opportunities do we have to close the benefit gaps that may be creating unnecessary class distinctions? How soon can we do it?

Should we consider a change of policy to establish local facility benefits rather than offer standardized corporate benefits? Which is better for our people?

What is the trend in our community towards an all-salaried operation? Are we all-salaried? If not, should we be?

How well do our employees understand our medical benefit program? How do we know?

What is our average turnaround time for the settlement of employee medical claims? How can we reduce it?

Is Long-term Disability (LTD) offered to all job classifications? Who pays for it—the organization or the employees? If employees do, what percentage have purchased it? Are we comfortable with that percentage?

Is everyone covered under the same life insurance policy? If not, why not? Have we considered a decreasing term policy?

What distinctions other than amount of insurance do we have in our life insurance benefit? What steps can be taken to eliminate these distinctions?

How many holidays a year do we have? What is the local norm? The national norm? The industry norm? How do we compare? Are our people satisfied with our holiday schedule?

Do we have floating holidays to incorporate local holidays? If not, why not?

Do we keep track of vacation time by hours rather than days?

Do we require proof of death when an employee uses the Death in Family benefit? If so, why do we? What message does it send?

How many days or hours off per year do we allow for sickness and/or personal business under our attendance policy? How does it compare to the local, industry and national norms?

Do we offer dental insurance? If not, why not? If so, is it preventive or restorative? If restorative, have we thought through its negative implications? Does our dental plan cover employees and dependents or employees only with an option for them to purchase dependent coverage at group rates?

Do our employees understand our retirement program? How do we know?

Does our retirement program have a defined benefit or a defined contribution or both? Have we considered the long-term economic ramifications of a defined benefit? Would a two-tiered retirement program better serve the needs of both employees and our organization? Have we explored the possibility? If not, why not?

What fringe benefits do we have? Do they improve or negate employee attitudes?

Should we consider eliminating a fringe benefit and using the money to improve a basic benefit?

How expensive are our benefits? What percentage of payroll are they equal to? Are we in line with our industry norms?

Why do our longer service people stay? How many of them are locked in by "golden handcuffs"? Do they have positive or negative attitudes?
Of our longer service employees who are locked in, what percent like their jobs? What percent don't? What problems does the latter group create?
Can we and should we make it easier for people to quit?
What basic problems do we have communicating and administering our benefits? How can we solve them?
Do we focus on communicating the benefit of the benefit?

APPENDIX B

A COMPARISON OF RESPONSES TO EMPLOYEE ATTITUDES SURVEY

(Percent Favorable Responses)

Items	Unionfree	Unionized	Difference*
Work is satisfying	82	76	[6]
Work group cooperation is o.k.	53	47	[6]
Opportunities to get ahead	67	55	[12]
Working conditions o.k.	77	60	[17]
Enough information on how we're doing	47	36	[11]
Confident of fair management	57	46	[11]
Retirement plan is o.k.	73	57	[16]
Sure of a job	79	73	[6]
Not too many rules, procedures	70	63	[7]
Have freedom to do job well	78	72	[6]
Can tell boss what I think	78	71	[7]
Proud to work for company	88	76	[12]
Paid fairly for kind of work	62	56	[6]
No outside job looked for	77	74	[3]
Favoritism no problem my area	64	55	[9]
Good use of employee abilities	65	59	[6]
Job leading to good future	56	47	[9]
Company better place this year	65	58	[7]
Know what is expected of me	91	88	[3]
Good insurance benefits	81	70	[11]
Average Favorable Response	71	62	[9]

*Differences of 2 points or more are significant.

APPENDIX C

WHAT CAUSES POOR ATTITUDES—A CHECKLIST OF TYPICAL EMPLOYEE COMPLAINTS

		Yes	No	?
1.	There is far too much favoritism with merit pay.	☐	☐	☐
2.	Forced bell-shaped distribution curves are used for performance ratings, so people are compared to other people instead of performance standards.	☐	☐	☐
3.	Managers get big bonuses for outshining their peers.	☐	☐	☐
4.	Industrial engineers have outdated mentalities.	☐	☐	☐
5.	Outside consultants are brought in to terrorize the staff.	☐	☐	☐
6.	Incredibly complex systems are used for job evaluation, and no one understands how they work, including the managers doing the evaluations.	☐	☐	☐
7.	Disruptive (Egocentric) employees are not terminated.	☐	☐	☐
8.	Ceiling-high walls separate all departments in the office and plant.	☐	☐	☐
9.	First shift people never meet second shift people.	☐	☐	☐
10.	Second shift people never meet third shift people.	☐	☐	☐
11.	The third shift never meets the first shift.	☐	☐	☐
12.	Fierce competition, to the point of rivalry, is instigated between departments under the guise of "improving productivity."	☐	☐	☐
13.	Attendance is more lenient for salaried than hourly.	☐	☐	☐
14.	Tuition reimbursement is available only to salaried.	☐	☐	☐
15.	Hourly employees are held to scheduled coffee and lunch breaks while salaried do as they please.	☐	☐	☐
16.	Office employees receive personal calls and use company phones, but production employees are denied personal calls and must use pay phones.	☐	☐	☐
17.	Some managers maintain a "speak only when spoken to or summoned" attitude.	☐	☐	☐
18.	The Open Door policy is preached but not practiced.	☐	☐	☐
19.	Quality Control people are paid less than other production personnel.	☐	☐	☐

		Yes	No	?
20.	Outside people are hired before attempts to promote from within.	☐	☐	☐
21.	Bean counters are allowed to influence employee relations policies.	☐	☐	☐
22.	People are laid off according to performance ratings rather than length of service.	☐	☐	☐
23.	Supervisors are not involved in hiring decisions.	☐	☐	☐
24.	Management plays games with the job bidding system.	☐	☐	☐
25.	Supervisors have different performance standards for different people doing the same job.	☐	☐	☐
26.	People doing the same jobs with the same expertise are paid different rates.	☐	☐	☐
27.	Managers say hello to people in some departments but ignore people in other departments.	☐	☐	☐
28.	Tool and die makers are treated like prima donnas.	☐	☐	☐
29.	MBAs with no practical experience are hired in at high salaries to supervise long-term experienced employees.	☐	☐	☐
30.	Management puts up with mediocre performers.	☐	☐	☐
31.	Top management puts up with poor managers.	☐	☐	☐
32.	Employees aren't allowed to solve their own problems.	☐	☐	☐
33.	Employees aren't recognized for solving problems or making improvements.	☐	☐	☐
34.	New policies, practices and decisions are forced on employees without their input.	☐	☐	☐
35.	Management seldom, if ever, announces any good news.	☐	☐	☐
36.	No one informs employees about the competition.	☐	☐	☐
37.	Management never announces an organizational philosophy or direction but expects employees to know what's going on.	☐	☐	☐
38.	Supervisors are allowed to run departments like fiefdoms.	☐	☐	☐
39.	Few all-employee or small-group meetings are held.	☐	☐	☐
40.	Supervisors aren't required to hold department meetings.	☐	☐	☐
41.	Supervisors and managers don't show actual performance ratings to individual employees.	☐	☐	☐
42.	Overtime is assigned unequally among departments and people.	☐	☐	☐
43.	Salaried are seldom, if ever, affected by layoffs.	☐	☐	☐
44.	Time clocks are required for hourly but not salaried.	☐	☐	☐

What Causes Poor Attitudes–A Checklist of Typical Employee Complaints

		Yes	No	?
45.	The office areas are better maintained than factory areas.	☐	☐	☐
46.	Managers try to roller skate through buffalo herds.	☐	☐	☐
47.	No close-in parking is reserved for the second shift.	☐	☐	☐
48.	Organizational goals are not announced or clarified.	☐	☐	☐
49.	Few people know what goes on in other departments.	☐	☐	☐
50.	Work groups are seldom allowed or asked to help each other.	☐	☐	☐
51.	Salaried people are paid for "Act of God" days but hourly people are docked.	☐	☐	☐
52.	Certain departments or individuals are granted "priority" on computers or word processors.	☐	☐	☐
53.	Management never asks employees for their opinions.	☐	☐	☐
54.	Top management doesn't have its act together, and hourly employees pay with their jobs for management incompetence.	☐	☐	☐
55.	Career development training sessions and workshops are held only for managers.	☐	☐	☐
56.	Management fails to respond to employee suggestions.	☐	☐	☐
57.	"Rank and file" employees are excluded from special task forces.	☐	☐	☐
58.	Outside contractors are hired when employees are laid off.	☐	☐	☐
59.	"Technically competent" supervisors and managers with poor people skills are retained even though they create problems.	☐	☐	☐
60.	Employee problems and requests are often ignored.	☐	☐	☐
61.	Management doesn't admit mistakes.	☐	☐	☐
62.	Management seldom, if ever, says "thank you" to people.	☐	☐	☐

APPENDIX D

A CHECKLIST OF OWNERSHIP PROCESS IDEAS

Here are some ideas to increase psychological ownership and decrease "we vs. they." Do you . . .

		Yes	No	?
1.	Get employees to write articles for your newsletter?	☐	☐	☐
2.	Run a draft of a new policy by all supervisors?	☐	☐	☐
3.	Have a group of employees sit in on management meetings?	☐	☐	☐
4.	Have regular meetings with questions and candid answers?	☐	☐	☐
5.	Test out bulletin board notices with employees before posting?	☐	☐	☐
6.	Have production employees make presentations to executives?	☐	☐	☐
7.	Have employees help design new plant or office layouts?	☐	☐	☐
8.	Ask employees which new holiday they want?	☐	☐	☐
9.	Have benefit users explain the benefits?	☐	☐	☐
10.	Have current employees do the new employee orientation?	☐	☐	☐
11.	Mix "rank and file" into a problem-solving task force?	☐	☐	☐
12.	Have one department explain to other departments what they do?	☐	☐	☐
13.	Send a nonmanagerial employee to visit with clients?	☐	☐	☐
14.	Ask employees to design their own performance appraisal system?	☐	☐	☐
15.	Have a task force do the community pay survey?	☐	☐	☐
16.	Take an employee along on a business trip to see a customer?	☐	☐	☐
17.	Have employees audit and redesign the job posting system?	☐	☐	☐
18.	Have an employee advisory group for the new handbook?	☐	☐	☐
19.	Have company T-shirts for employees (and kids)?	☐	☐	☐

Making Unions Unnecessary

		Yes	No	?
20.	Have employees work with customers on technical problems?	☐	☐	☐
21.	Have employees make presentations to financial analysts?	☐	☐	☐
22.	Get employee input on advertising campaigns?	☐	☐	☐
23.	Let employees help select consultants?	☐	☐	☐
24.	Use an employee task force to overhaul the attendance policy?	☐	☐	☐
25.	Ask employees to set up dress code rules?	☐	☐	☐
26.	Let supervisors use executive conference rooms for meetings?	☐	☐	☐
27.	Put employee testimonials in your job ads?	☐	☐	☐
28.	Have the work group approve all new hires in advance?	☐	☐	☐
29.	Have employees design the new-employee orientation program?	☐	☐	☐
30.	Have employees identify their own training needs?	☐	☐	☐
31.	Have supervisors identify their own training needs?	☐	☐	☐
32.	Have employees identify managers' training needs?	☐	☐	☐
33.	Have a task force work on containing medical insurance costs?	☐	☐	☐
34.	Have individuals put their names in the package with the product?	☐	☐	☐
35.	Have employees give purchasing agents opinions about purchases?	☐	☐	☐
36.	Have a special annual report for employees?	☐	☐	☐
37.	Have supervisors participate in the selection of new supervisors?	☐	☐	☐
38.	Tell employees of news before you tell the media?	☐	☐	☐
39.	Have production employees meet directly with quality control?	☐	☐	☐
40.	Use in-house talent rather than subcontractors?	☐	☐	☐
41.	Ask individuals to teach managers how to operate a machine?	☐	☐	☐
42.	Use an ad hoc committee to audit procedure manuals?	☐	☐	☐
43.	Bring employees in on long-range planning?	☐	☐	☐
44.	Have employees sit in on budget reviews?	☐	☐	☐
45.	Have machinists evaluate new machines before purchase?	☐	☐	☐
46.	Have toolmakers assist engineers on design projects?	☐	☐	☐
47.	Have programmers meet with employees on report design?	☐	☐	☐
48.	Have a task force evaluate your security system?	☐	☐	☐

A Checklist of Ownership Process Ideas

		Yes	No	?
49.	Have a committee plan the cafeteria menu?	☐	☐	☐
50.	Publish testimonials from employees who benefit from benefits?	☐	☐	☐
51.	Educate employees on the free enterprise system?	☐	☐	☐
52.	Discuss unions before they show up?	☐	☐	☐
53.	Hold an open house for employees' families?	☐	☐	☐
54.	Let a committee arrange the service recognition function?	☐	☐	☐
55.	Get employee input on selecting new uniforms?	☐	☐	☐
56.	Make business cards available for everyone?	☐	☐	☐
57.	Invite employees to shareholder meetings?	☐	☐	☐
58.	Hold a spontaneous meeting whenever a goal is reached?	☐	☐	☐
59.	Call all employees by their first names?	☐	☐	☐
60.	Have "first come, first served" parking?	☐	☐	☐
61.	Let everyone use the same entrance?	☐	☐	☐
62.	Pay everyone on the same dates?	☐	☐	☐
63.	Ask for employee referrals on new hires?	☐	☐	☐
64.	Have employees rate their supervisors' job performance?	☐	☐	☐
65.	Provide a common coffee break area for everyone?	☐	☐	☐
66.	Have an "open mind" inside the "open door"?	☐	☐	☐
67.	Get personally involved in cleanup and housekeeping?	☐	☐	☐
68.	Hold spontaneous meetings to solve problems?	☐	☐	☐
69.	Provide real-time continuous feedback on quality?	☐	☐	☐
70.	Circulate or post positive letters from customers?	☐	☐	☐
71.	Circulate or post negative letters from customers?	☐	☐	☐
72.	Let employees be tour guides for visitors?	☐	☐	☐
73.	Have slogans or logos about your products/services/customers?	☐	☐	☐
74.	Ask employees to evaluate training programs?	☐	☐	☐
75.	Let employees "decorate" their work areas?	☐	☐	☐
76.	Post the names and affiliations of visitors?	☐	☐	☐
77.	Publish brief biographies and photos of new employees?	☐	☐	☐
78.	Let an employee use your phone for a personal emergency?	☐	☐	☐
79.	Have the same quality art in the cafeteria as in your office?	☐	☐	☐
80.	Phone an employee or family member who is in the hospital?	☐	☐	☐
81.	Design facilities that intermingle production and office areas?	☐	☐	☐

		Yes	No	?
82.	Call a meeting to admit a mistake?	☐	☐	☐
83.	Have employees make presentations at the shareholders' meeting?	☐	☐	☐
84.	Post rate ranges for all jobs?	☐	☐	☐
85.	Post attendance records, including your own?	☐	☐	☐
86.	Have a "letter to the editor" section in your newsletter?	☐	☐	☐
87.	Have sales meet with employees about customer problems?	☐	☐	☐
88.	Explain free enterprise to the children of employees?	☐	☐	☐
89.	Talk with an employee in the hall, for no reason?	☐	☐	☐
90.	Make a speech without a prepared script?	☐	☐	☐
91.	Send a technician to a professional society conference—in Hawaii?	☐	☐	☐
92.	Open up "management development" seminars to nonmanagers?	☐	☐	☐
93.	Have employees help consultants design benefits?	☐	☐	☐
94.	Have employees survey community attitudes about the company?	☐	☐	☐
95.	Feature employees in brochures to customers?	☐	☐	☐
96.	Have humor in the newsletter? In speeches? Memos? Life?	☐	☐	☐
97.	Hold meetings between customers and quality control inspectors?	☐	☐	☐
98.	Feature employees in your annual report to shareholders?	☐	☐	☐
99.	Have a company song?	☐	☐	☐
100.	Do something spontaneously outrageous?	☐	☐	☐
101.	Ask employees to make up a list like this?	☐	☐	☐

APPENDIX E

A CHECKLIST FOR YOUR PAY SYSTEM

How well does your organization's pay system work? Here's a list of questions to help you put your pay system in perspective:

	Yes	No	?
• Does management focus more on achieving statistical equity in setting pay rates or on having positive employee attitudes about being paid fairly—perceived equity?	☐	☐	☐
• Is there a clear, concise description of your pay system in the handbook, or is there only abstract terminology such as "above average"?	☐	☐	☐
• Does your organization have external equity with other community organizations for similar skill levels? Has this been explained to all the people?	☐	☐	☐
• Were the supervisors or any of their workgroups sufficiently involved in preparing job descriptions, so they find them accurate and useful?	☐	☐	☐
• If people were to ask supervisors why certain jobs are in particular job grades, could most supervisors give a convincing, understandable answer?	☐	☐	☐
• Are there so many pay classes that you have excessive range overlap to the point that people are confused as to why lower grade jobs pay more money than higher graded ones?	☐	☐	☐
• Is the progression time through the rate ranges far in excess of the actual learning curves on the jobs in that rate range?	☐	☐	☐
• Do you have a service premium to recognize the value of long service, experience and loyalty to the organization?	☐	☐	☐
• Does each different job have a specific set of performance standards, unique to the job, designed with the involvement of supervisors and workers?	☐	☐	☐
• Does each job's performance standards specify speed and accuracy for the critical tasks the job comprises?	☐	☐	☐

	Yes	No	?

- Does your organization's performance rating system measure performance for each individual versus job standards, or is the bell-shaped curve being used to force person-to-person appraisal? ☐ ☐ ☐
- Do you expect top performance from all individuals in order to receive a pay increase, or does management believe in accepting varying performance levels? ☐ ☐ ☐
- Do the scattergrams of pay vs. length of service for each job classification indicate that your organization pays for length of service rather than merit? ☐ ☐ ☐
- If a difference was revealed between policy and practice by the scattergram analysis, has a resolution been made to adopt an automatic progression system? ☐ ☐ ☐
- If no essential correlation of service and pay is determined by the scattergram, has the merit system been explained to employees? ☐ ☐ ☐
- Are there nonsupervisory employees with higher W-2 earnings than their supervisors? ☐ ☐ ☐
- When annual or semiannual general schedule pay increases are made, does each rate range receive the amount of change appropriate to the survey market price? ☐ ☐ ☐
- Do managers recognize that annual pay increases of any type (general rate increases, automatic progression or merit increases) come so infrequently that there is little effect on productivity? ☐ ☐ ☐
- Would a monthly/quarterly group productivity improvement bonus system be appropriate? ☐ ☐ ☐

APPENDIX F

THE INGREDIENTS OF A PAY SYSTEM

These suggestions will help your company create a new pay system for a start-up operation or completely overhaul an unworkable design. It begins with an overview, then details the steps, using an objectives, strategies, and tactics approach. Critical questions are raised in each step.

Overview:

Establish Policy

Objective: What is going to be your competitive position?
What surveys will be used? Are they appropriate survey companies?
Who is in charge of pay administration?

Establish Job Structure and Relationships

Horizontal comparisons across the facility? Vertical relationships within the facility?

Establish Strategy

What are you trying to accomplish (for a single group or total facility)?

Determine Tactics to Establish System and Pay Rates

How many vertical levels will there be? How wide will the ranges be? What is the overlap between ranges?
What determines movement in range? (merit, automatic, skills)? When and how will ranges be adjusted? How will individual reviews and raises be done?

Establish Systematic Communication Process

Pay policy and concepts for the organization.
Involvement of supervisors and employees. Pay system, structure and ranges.
Survey base and changes.
Survey results and internal impact.

Policy Questions:

- Is the competitive position a policy or a goal? That is, is it what you will absolutely do (policy) or what you hope to be able to do (goal)? It makes a big difference in later decisions.
- What are the appropriate survey companies? Same industry or same skills?
- Who will get the survey data? What is already available?
- Is the survey based on job to job, benchmark jobs only, roughly comparable jobs, competitive jobs?
- What survey information do you want—the other companies' total structure, paid average, number of employees by rate?

Structure Questions:

Fair Labor Standards Act Requirements

Exempt classifications:

- What jobs fall into executive, administrative, professional, outside sales? Can these jobs meet the FLSA tests?
- Is there a guaranteed salary?

Non-exempt classifications:

- How will hours be recorded?
- What is the work week?
- What about minimum wage, overtime pay, shift differentials?
- Is an all-salaried system desirable?

Horizontal Structure

- What jobs fall into the same family or class? Manufacturing and Production? Office and Clerical? Exempt? Management?
- How will first-line supervision fit in and be paid?

Job Titles

- Will specific titles be used for each job, or generic titles that cut across the facility or company?

Vertical Structure

- How many pay grades/classes should there be? Can it be held to a minimum, such as five or fewer?
- Will this be determined by formal job evaluation or by involvement of supervisors and other employees to get consensus?
- Is a project team approach desirable?

Range Determinations

- Should there be a range with a minimum and maximum rate? Or should there be a single rate for each grade?
- Will the maximum rate be for "fully qualified" based on the survey?
- Should ranges be average or would the "lead and lag" approach be better?
- Will the minimum rate be set as a percentage of the maximum rate? And how much below?
- What is the "learning curve" on each job, and will that be the basis for the minimum to maximum spread?
- When an employee "tops out," will there be a premium added on for merit, service, versatility, leaders and shift? Should this be a percent added on, or cents/dollars or a bonus?
- When the ranges are adjusted, will individuals within the ranges be adjusted automatically?

Progression Through the Range

Merit Questions:

- Will there be steps or not (only a minimum, maximum and midpoint)?
- How will performance appraisals tie in?
- Will there be fixed amounts and varied timing of increase, or varied amounts and fixed timing?
- How well can job performance be rated? Is it more subjective or objective?

Automatic Questions:

- What will be the fixed steps or increments up the range?
- If the progression is based on service, is it "up or out"?

Versatility and Skills Questions:

- How will the required skills be measured?
- Will the increments be based on a predetermined number of skills or a premium per skill?
- Can the versatility/skills increases be built into the basic automatic step progressions?

Promotion to Next Grade

- What are the historical lines of progression?
- How are promotional pay increases handled if there are rate range overlaps between the maximum of one and the minimum of the next?
- Will promotions be based on a "bidding" system, a "seniority" system or on the individual? And how much weight do merit, skills and service get?

IV

REFERENCES

REFERENCES

Clare W. Graves, "Deterioration of Work Standards," *Harvard Business Review*, September-October, 1966.

Clare W. Graves, "Human Nature Prepares for a Momentous Leap," *The Futurist*, April, 1974.

Clare W. Graves, "Levels of Existence: An Open System of Values," *Journal of Humanistic Psychology*, Fall, 1970.

Charles L. Hughes and Lewis H. Aronson, "A Systems Approach to Gainsharing," CVR, Inc., Dallas, Texas, manuscript.

Charles L. Hughes and Vincent S. Flowers, "Why Employees Stay Is More Critical Than Why They Leave," *Personnel Journal*, October, 1987.

Charles L. Hughes and Wayne L. Wright, "Make Pay Plans Work for the People They Pay," *Personnel Journal*, May 1989.

Robert F. Mager and Peter Pipe, *Analyzing Performance Problems or 'You Really Oughta Wanna,'* Fearon Publishers, Belmont, California, 1970.

Allan Mogensen (p6-29 in now-chapt 7)

Wayne L. Wright, *East Meets West*, CVR, Dallas, Texas, 1987.

Wayne L. Wright, "Overcoming Barriers to Productivity," *Personnel Journal*, February, 1987.